GODDARD PARENTING GUIDES

Winning Ways to Learn

Ages 6, 7 & 8

600 Great Ideas for Children

Samuel J. Meisels, Ed.D.
Charlotte Stetson, M.Ed. ✦ Dorothea B. Marsden, M.Ed.

GODDARD PRESS
380 MADISON AVENUE
NEW YORK, NY 10017

Book design by Jenkins Group, Inc.

Manufactured in the United States of America.

PUBLISHER'S CATALOGING-IN-PUBLICATION DATA

Meisels, Samuel J.

Winning ways to learn: ages 6, 7 & 8: 600 great ideas for children / Samuel J. Meisels, Charlotte Stetson, Dorothea B. Marsden.

ISBN 0-9666397-7-4

1. Early childhood education—Parent participation—Handbooks, manuals, etc.   2. Education, Primary—Handbooks, manuals, etc. I. Stetson, Charlotte. II. Marsden, Dorothea.   III. Title. IV. Series.

LB1139.35 .P37 M46   2000   00-102858

372/ .241—dc21   CIP

To the parents and teachers who have inspired us and taught us so much.

Acknowledgments

✦

Thanks,

To the A. L. Mailman Family Foundation for supporting this work with a generous grant;

To the University of Michigan for providing the setting that nurtured this work;

To the Joyce Foundation for their assistance in piloting these books;

To the parents who participated in focus groups, read these pages, allowed us to quote them in this book, and offered us the benefit of their wisdom and experience;

To our colleagues Judy Jablon and Margo Dichtelmiller, whose contributions to the Work Sampling System® Omnibus Guidelines inspired the organization of the domains and content of these guides;

To Jackie Post for planning, organizing, leading, and summarizing the parent focus groups, and to Ruth Piker, for assisting with the focus groups;

To Mary Brandau, Principal, Kettering Elementary, Willow Run, MI; Kathy Scarnecchia, Principal, Dicken Elementary, Ann Arbor, MI; Lori Fidler, Family Resource Coordinator, Perry Child Development Center, Ypsilanti, MI; and Jane Williams, Director, Willow Run Head Start, Ypsilanti, MI; for facilitating the focus groups;

To Laura Yale and her colleagues at Fairview Elementary School in Milwaukee, WI; Colleen Krajcik, Clarke Street School, Milwaukee, WI; Lesley Straley, Townshend Elementary School, Townshend, VT; Nancy Gerace and Dennis Bell, West Gate Elementary School, West Palm Beach, FL; Nancy Hoff, Gwendolyn Beurnett, and Theresa Torres, Arnn Elementary School, Camp Zama Army Base, Japan; Sam and Ann Morse, Amherst, MA; Eileen Harris, Charlotte County Public Schools, Port Charlotte, FL; Patricia Stevens, Principal, West Early Childhood Center, Midland, TX: Barbara Trube, Principal, Bunche Early Childhood Center, Midland, TX; for reviewing early versions, commenting on them, and obtaining feedback from parents and teachers;

To Patty Humphrey, for her patient, tireless, skillful, and dedicated attention to producing countless versions of these materials, and for coordinating the myriad details that helped bring this project to fruition; and

To Barbara Turvett, whose careful, sensitive, and imaginative editing, and knowledge about children and families touched every page and every idea in these books.

Contents

✦

✦

WINNING WAYS TO LEARN FOR 7-YEAR-OLDS

✦

WINNING WAYS TO LEARN FOR 8-YEAR-OLDS

CHAPTER 1

A Winning Approach for Families and Children

✦

Welcome to **Winning Ways to Learn**. This book is filled with ideas you can use to help your child learn as you go about your everyday activities. You will find that the **Winning Ways to Learn** approach is easy, it's fun, and it works!

This book will help your child become a successful and enthusiastic learner by showing you how to support him* in developing the skills and attributes that are important in the preschool years.

Winning Ways to Learn differs from other teaching aids because its focus goes beyond drill and practice. Research shows us that those children who love to learn and who are also good learners share several important attributes:

They believe in themselves.

They feel competent.

They aren't afraid to take reasonable risks and to fail.

They understand that working toward a goal will eventually pay off.

They are curious and inquisitive about ideas, objects, people, and the world.

The are able to conceptualize and represent ideas.

They find pleasure in the process as well as in the product of their work.

---

* "Him" and "her" are used interchangeably throughout this book. All of the ideas and activities that are described can be used with either boys or girls.

Winning Ways to Learn is intended to help you develop these attributes in your child. Although acquiring factual information is central to learning, it is only one component of a complex and multifaceted process. A child's attitudes are vitally important, too. A simple activity, such as weighing and measuring different household items, not only involves numbers, which must be memorized, but also teaches spatial and conceptual skills.

Activities such as the measuring exercise above can also be turned into games. Find the biggest window! Which box of cereal is heaviest? How many doors do we have? This, too, is important. We know that the learning and emotional centers of the brain are closely related. Having a good time clearly enhances the process of learning. It also makes children want to learn even more. Like the rest of us, children want to do more of what they enjoy.

The activities in this book cover *all* the bases. They will help your child learn a great deal of specific information. But just as important, they will help build a strong foundation for learning in your child. Curiosity, perseverance, higher order thinking, creativity, imagination, problem-solving—these and many more skills and attributes are all part of the total learning process.

As you will see in this book, you can help your child build this foundation as you introduce her to the possibilities for learning that abound in everyday life. **Winning Ways to Learn** will help you find countless ways to turn ordinary activities into potent learning opportunities.

Using this book as a guide will also help to deepen your respect for your child as a learner. You will gain a better understanding of how your child learns at school and home and how he can become an even more successful learner. In addition, the experience and information offered here can increase the pleasure you experience when spending time with your child. You will enjoy being with him during some wonderful moments of learning. A key to learning for all of us—especially young children—is an openness to change. As parents, **Winning Ways to Learn** can help you become more aware of how much your child is learning and changing.

THE BRIDGE BETWEEN HOME AND SCHOOL

Winning Ways to Learn is more than a learn-at-home primer, valuable as that may be. It will also help build a bridge between school and home, even if schooling takes place at home. This book will help you:

✦ Understand some activities that occur in the classroom.

✦ Notice what your child does at home that reflects what he has learned in school.

✦ Know what to do at home to support and advance your child's learning.

Armed with this information, you can easily create an enjoyable and effective learning environment at home that will consistently support what's being learned and taught in school.

The parent connection is extremely important here. Studies show that when parents are involved with their children's school-related learning efforts, children do better in school. Part of this is the additional time spent on learning. But a big part is a caring parent's personal input, attention, and responsiveness. You are irreplaceable. Your initiative, encouragement, patience, enthusiasm, and praise cannot be provided by computers or video games. Your involvement will further your child's motivation at school and his learning-to-learn skills in ways nothing else can. But don't worry. Done properly, this is not burdensome. The **Winning Ways to Learn** activities will become an enjoyable part of daily living, not an extra demand on your schedule.

WHAT'S IN *WINNING WAYS TO LEARN*

This book is divided into three major sections, one for each year, ages six through eight. The section for each age covers the following seven major learning areas:

1. Personal and Social Development

2. Language and Literacy

3. Mathematical Thinking

4. Scientific Thinking

5. Social Studies

6. The Arts

7. Physical Development and Health

Each learning area begins with a discussion of what a child of that age should be learning. This is followed by a section labeled *From School to Home*, which tells you how a teacher might help your child learn about a particular area, and how your child might demonstrate this learning at home. The goal is to help you better understand why your child's teacher may use certain activities and how some of your child's naturally occurring questions, ideas, or activities at home are extensions of what he has learned at school.

For example, if you visit your child's classroom, you may find a jar filled with hard candies, marbles, or buttons. You might also see children go to the jar, write down a number on a piece of paper, and then put the number in a nearby envelope. Why did the teacher put a jar of candy in the middle of the classroom? What are the students learning?

The teacher filled the jar with hard candies or other objects to help children learn that volume can be filled by numerous small objects and to teach them to estimate volume and contents. Sure, there are other ways to teach this. But a jar of candy is a good way to capture children's attention, and it is easy for children to make the connection between this type of problem and other problems that they might have to solve, or estimates they need to make in everyday life.

At home you might find your child guessing how many cookies are in a package you just brought back from the store, or how many raisins are left in the box, or how much the dog or cat weighs. Like the classroom tasks, these activities also involve estimation. Conversations about them may take place at home after your child's teacher begins to focus on this skill. This book will help you understand how conversations such as these support your child's learning at home and at school.

To help you do this, you will find sections throughout the book called *It's Your Turn*. These sections include over 600 activities and ideas—more than 200 for each age—that you can enjoy with your child. All involve simple materials or experiences that come directly from home, family, and neighborhood. Suggestions include materials to keep on hand, things to do with your child, books to read, and trips to take.

You don't have to buy expensive toys or equipment, and you don't have to know more than you know already as a parent or family member. All you need is a desire to nurture your child's learning and a willingness to engage her in activities that will add to what she can do already.

As you read the suggested activities for each age level, you will see a clear pattern of year-to-year growth on all fronts. You will also find many ways in which a skill in one area supports growth in other areas. For example, conceptual thinking in some of the social studies activities builds skills for math and science, too. In particular, the strengths developed in the personal and social area affect your child's approach to learning in all other areas.

THE SOURCE OF *WINNING WAYS TO LEARN*

Winning Ways to Learn is the product of over twenty years of research, development, and testing. It is a direct descendant of the **Work Sampling System**®, an innovative program used by tens of thousands of teachers nationwide for assessing children's skills, knowledge, behavior, and accomplishments. The **Work Sampling System** was developed to help teachers of 3-year-olds through fifth-graders observe, document, and assess children's achievements within the rich and varied contexts of learning. Specifically, it was designed to tell teachers how *well* students are doing by documenting *what* children are doing.

The **Work Sampling System** helps teachers keep track of the many skills and behaviors that are not covered in typical achievement tests. It includes not only the academic subjects of math, science, and reading, but also many subjects, skills, and aptitudes that are central to the learning process, including social skills that are so important to working well with adults and other children.

The activities in **Winning Ways to Learn** are based on those in the **Work Sampling System** that are used to gauge children's performance and that have helped improve children's academic achievement. Like the **Work Sampling System**, the activities in **Winning Ways to Learn** cover the full range of skills that children are expected to develop, and they recognize and appeal to a wide variety of children's and families' interests.

These activities will help you foster your child's special interests and favorite activities. They will also help encourage growth in areas in which your child is only beginning to explore or in which she needs extra help.

BE CREATIVE!

When it comes to your child, you are the expert. That's because, like all concerned parents, you know more about your child than anyone else: what makes her happy or sad, what is difficult for her, and what she enjoys.

The activities in this book can easily be expanded by you and your child. Be creative. Write down new ideas as they come to you, and ask your child and other family members to think of new things to do as well. You will find that some activities will become favorites, and you and your child will go back to them often.

You will soon see how some of the simple, everyday things you do with your child can support her educational growth and can build on what she is learning at school or in other educational settings. These experiences will help your child know more, do more, think more carefully, and use her knowledge and skills more effectively. In short, your child will gain a keener sense of the world and how to succeed in it.

Happy learning!

Winning Ways to Learn
for 6-Year-Olds

CHAPTER 2

Personal and Social Development

✦

The message is clear: When children of any age have confidence in themselves—when they believe in their own ability to learn things—they *will* learn. This feeling of self-worth can promote their success in the school environment, not only in the way they tackle the three Rs, but in the way they relate to other children and teachers. And strong relationships with peers and teachers can have a positive effect on children's overall school success. For these reasons, personal and social development represents a vital component of learning. Children's growth in this area can be viewed through their:

Self-concept and self-control

Approach to learning

Interactions with others

SELF-CONCEPT AND SELF-CONTROL

What makes first-graders confident? Knowing that important adults appreciate and like them, getting praise from adults, having rewarding friendships with other children, being independent, and having opportunities to try out their ideas all contribute to positive feelings about themselves. Six-year-olds are going through some dramatic developmental changes. They want to take part in creating rules and they want to make sure everyone follows them. They want to feel responsible and grown-up enough to use many of the same tools, equipment, and materials they see adults using. With instruction and guidance, they can be successful. And first-graders want to know what's happening at all times; they'll need advanced notice when changes in routine are necessary.

FROM SCHOOL TO HOME

Your child's teacher promotes your first-grader's confidence and competence in many ways. Your child grows in self-assurance when she does classroom activities and projects independently; her teacher gives simple directions and your child carries them out. She now chooses her own partners and activities. She collects tools and materials for a project, uses them, and returns them when she's finished. She's able to look at a schedule posted in class and check it throughout the day to see what comes next. And she carries out classroom jobs responsibly.

Her growing independence and self-assurance enable her to try difficult tasks repeatedly at home, but she still needs encouragement from you. She is able to find the materials she needs and then complete a simple craft project, such as making a mask, a mobile, or a birthday card. She may ask to borrow markers and pencils from an older sibling; she will now put them back when she is finished using them. Your six-year-old will do her family jobs with only one or two reminders. And she'll now more regularly say *please, thank you, excuse me*, and *I'm sorry*.

IT'S YOUR TURN

To foster your six-year-old's growing sense of self:

✦ **Show your joy**—when you talk and play with your child.

✦ **Empower her with independence.** Suggest activities that allow her to be safely self-reliant: making her own sandwich for lunch, walking to a friend's apartment down the hall, using the hose to water the garden.

✦ **Give her important things to do.** Help your child learn to be responsible by giving her meaningful household chores: feeding the family pet, watering plants, putting away laundry.

✦ **Help her do her thing.** Find time to share projects that interest your child, such as creating and sending a beautiful card to her grandparent.

✦ **Applaud her can-do attitude.** Praise your child's efforts to be independent and take charge of things: "Thank you so much for getting out the things we need to make your lunch!"

✦ **Create a chart together**. Ask your child to keep track of the jobs she completes each day. She'll gain a sense of mastery as she charts and sees clearly all that she has accomplished.

✦ **Ask your child for help.** Let her prepare meals with you—tossing the salad, measuring and mixing ingredients.

✦ **Celebrate her successes.** Do something special to mark your child's accomplishments and "firsts," such as riding her two-wheeler without training wheels or remembering to feed her pet for a whole month without reminders. When you honor her actions in this way, you bolster her self-esteem and encourage further independent activity.

✦ **Give her some power.** Ask your child to help create family rules, and help her write them on a sign to put in a special place.

✦ **Remind her about public rules**—how to behave at the library, the grocery store, a place of worship, school, a friend's house.

✦ **Prep her for responsibility.** Give your child clear instructions about using and caring for someone else's things.

✦ **If you need to make changes, tell her.** Make your child's schedule and routines as predictable as possible. When changes are necessary, tell your child about them in advance, if possible. This will give her a chance to think about and then ease herself into the shift.

APPROACH TO LEARNING

First-graders are intensely curious and eager to learn about new things. But too much sitting and listening may dampen this enthusiasm. Six-year-olds are pretty clear about what they want to do and how they want to do it, and choices are important to them. They can be flexible and inventive when they work on projects or play games. They'll try different ways to solve a problem and will ask for help when they get stuck. Their attention span is growing—especially when it comes to activities they have chosen themselves—although they're still likely to start more projects than they finish.

From School to Home

The classroom environment offers your six-year-old opportunities to follow his special interests. He makes decisions about what to write about during writing time, which math game to play, which books to read during quiet time, and who to work with in the block area. He may return to the science center or to a puzzle three days in a row to finish a long-term project. He may go with a small group to the library, watch a particular video, or talk to a visitor in the classroom. He asks questions and shares ideas about whatever the class is studying, whether it is animals, cities, farms, or space travel. In his enthusiasm, he may bring books, pictures, or objects from home that relate to the study project.

At home your child may develop a special interest in a specific topic: rocks, insects, music, animals. He'll want to follow up on school activities, such as science experiments or math activities. You'll be amazed by his many creative ideas. He may develop a unique approach to making his bed or cleaning his room. Or he may use a rock for a hammer, mix red and yellow paint to get orange, and repair broken objects with glue or tape. Your child will also want to offer his good ideas during family mealtime discussions.

"I like the idea that children have choices and are able to problem-solve with a little guidance."

It's Your Turn

To nurture your child's growing sense of discovery:

+ **Show him your interest.** Let your child see your enthusiasm for his passions: Ask questions; help him organize his projects or decide how to display them.

+ **Support his choices.** Help your child follow through on something he wants to do, such as being the caregiver for the family pet.

+ **Suggest possible solutions:** "Would this cardboard box help you make your puppet theater?"

+ **Solicit solutions:** "Can you help me figure out how we can wash the dog?"

+ **Cheer his "stick-to-itiveness."** Praise your child's growing persistence and patience: "You've been making great progress on that cardboard-box house you started last week!"

+ **Model a love of learning.** Be a curious learner yourself: Notice and talk about things; read books to your child on topics both you and he enjoy.

+ **Let him share your passion.** Involve your child in *your* special interests, such as gardening, cooking, sports news, astronomy, playing board games, and so on.

+ **Go places together.** Plan excursions—visiting a museum, going to a car show, attending local musical presentations, roaming community fairs.

+ **Support ingenuity.** Encourage your child to think of more than one way to do things.

+ **Get excited about school.** Let your child know you think school and learning are important by: asking questions about his day at school; helping with homework; looking at the work he brings home; going to school for conferences and special events; writing notes to his teacher.

INTERACTIONS WITH OTHERS

Most six-year-olds are social beings—friends are very important to them. Often, however, conflict arises between what they want for themselves and what they know is best for making and keeping a friend. Helping, sharing, taking turns, compromising, and solving disagreements come easily for some first-graders, while others will need extra support from adults. Six-year-olds tend to be extremely competitive, and they also love games. Cooperative games that allow everybody to feel like a winner work very well at this age. (*The Cooperative Sports and Games Book* by Terry Orlick is an excellent resource.)

Six-year-olds are beginning to learn how to be sensitive to the feelings of others. It is difficult for them to understand how someone else feels, especially when they do not agree with the other person. They need adults to model respectful ways of solving conflicts, to talk things over with them, and to give them praise when they've tried to settle a conflict calmly.

FROM SCHOOL TO HOME

The first-grade classroom provides your child with many opportunities for social growth. She works with groups on school activities and projects, listening, sharing ideas, and cleaning up with others. She plays games in small groups, following the rules and waiting for turns. Her social sense broadens through books, too, as she reads and talks about stories in which the characters settle conflicts. Your first-grader learns from one-on-one interactions, as well: She may accompany an injured classmate to the nurse, or she may go to an adult or another child on the playground for help in settling a problem.

Around the neighborhood you'll see your child wait her turn and follow the rules when playing with other children. She may come in from playing with a friend to talk to you about a disagreement they are having: "Dad, Jody and I each want to be in the hammock alone. What should we do?" At her house or a friend's apartment she'll compromise or engage in give-and-take with her pal by, for example, playing with Legos even though she'd rather draw. Demonstrating growing compassion, your child will do special things for a sibling who is sick, such as offering toys or a snack.

IT'S YOUR TURN

To help your child sharpen social skills:

+ **Plan a playdate.** Show interest in your child's friendships by arranging for her to play with other children; stay nearby to help if problems come up.

+ **Compliment her social skills.** Praise and support your child's successful friendships.

+ **Read books about friendship.** Your local children's librarian will have lots of suggestions. And don't forget the great classic, *Charlotte's Web* by E. B. White.

+ **Go for more than the win.** Encourage your child to play games and sports, but help her focus on learning new skills, cheering on the other players, and working as a team rather than just winning or losing.

+ **Encourage empathy.** Find examples in real life or in books that show children who need caring and sensitivity, and talk about these children with your child.

+ **Chat with her.** Include your child in conversations so she learns how to listen, ask questions, and respond to what others say.

+ **Teach her to use "I" statements**—to resolve conflicts: "I don't like it when you pretend to shoot me. Please stop."

+ **...and other words to settle issues.** Show your child how to settle a disagreement by talking about differences of opinion. For example, she could say, "I know you want to play at the park and I want to play at my house. So, let's take turns: This Saturday we'll play at the park, and next Saturday we'll play at my house."

+ **Let her settle her own disputes.** Give your child suggestions for settling conflicts, but avoid being the umpire and working them out for her.

+ **Talk over upsets when they are over.** Avoid punishing your child for getting angry in a conflict. Instead, talk with her after she has calmed down about ways to handle the problem differently the next time.

+ **Brainstorm.** Together, come up with several ways to resolve real or pretend conflicts so your child sees that it is possible to find different solutions for a single issue.

+ **Discuss fictional conflicts.** When people have disagreements in the books you read or the television programs you view together, talk about how they deal with them.

+ **Find alternatives to violence.** Talk openly with your child about the violence she sees on the news or in newspapers and the possibility of thinking of other ways to deal with conflicts.

CHAPTER 3

Language and Literacy

✦

Letters, letter sounds, books, and reading receive a lot of attention in the first-grade classroom. Every day your child listens to stories read aloud and takes part in discussions about them—which part she liked best, which character reminded her of someone she knows, how the problems raised by the story were solved, and so on. Many other first-grade activities involve reading: listening to "big books" with the whole class, or taped stories with a small group in a listening center; playing card games that require matching pictures and words, or board games with simple written directions to follow; using computer programs that involve sounding out letters or combinations of letters; putting on puppet shows or skits about favorite stories; reading "early readers" with the teacher's guidance; reading quietly, alone, or with a partner. Even much of the artwork in a first-grade classroom is about the books that six-year-olds know and love.

Children also develop many language skills in addition to reading and writing. They learn these skills in the same way they learn to talk, naturally and slowly, getting closer and closer to the standard and more sophisticated forms of language as they grow older. First-graders' progress in this important area can be seen in:

Listening and speaking

Literature and reading

Writing and spelling

LISTENING AND SPEAKING

For first-graders, listening and speaking are closely connected. Children take in a lot of new information through listening, and they love to share what they know! Six-year-olds listen well when they are interested or amused, but they lose interest when a topic is not meaningful to them. They listen to directions, but they may forget or become sidetracked while carrying them out. The language of first-graders seems to grow and improve with each day. They are learning many new words and expressions and are increasingly able to put their ideas into words. They are discovering that words are useful for learning, socializing, and communicating ideas.

FROM SCHOOL TO HOME

Your child has many occasions to work on his language skills in his first-grade classroom. He listens to the teacher give instructions and then follows them without reminders. He listens to classmates' stories and asks questions afterwards. Your six-year-old may retell a story in his own words or make up rhymes, songs, and riddles to share with the class. He is learning and using new vocabulary as part of something he is studying. In classroom discussions, he is now able to offer his own ideas.

At home your child listens intently to stories read aloud. He also listens to and asks questions of a family member who is telling about an event. You'll notice that he has important things to say during family discussions. He can now retell or make up jokes. You'll also hear him use appropriate words to express feelings, problems, experiences, and questions and respond to things you say: For instance, he'll find items in the grocery store that you've asked him to look for.

IT'S YOUR TURN

To encourage your child's verbal give-and-take:

+ **Read and chat.** Ask questions or talk with your child about a story when you finish reading it to him.

+ **Show him how *you* listen.** Model good listening habits when your child talks: Pay attention, ask questions, make related comments.

+ **Make sure he's in on the plan.** Find out whether your child understands a set of directions before he tries to carry them out, and patiently repeat them if he did not understand or if he forgot.

+ **Explain the game.** As you read game directions to your child, explain them in different words, step-by-step.

+ **Play listening games**—such as "Hum That Tune," in which one person hums a tune and others try to guess what song it is.

+ **...or try "add-on stories"**—in which players take turns adding on one word to a story.

+ **Train his ear.** Listen to music or books on tape.

+ **Listen to the world together.** Take listening walks around the neighborhood, and keep a list of everything you hear.

+ **Tell him to tell it.** Encourage your child to make up his own stories to tell to you.

+ **Question his answers.** Use prompts, such as, "Try to explain that again," or, "Tell me more about that," if you do not fully understand what your child is saying.

+ **Promote his public voice.** Give your child chances to talk with a variety of people, either in person or on the telephone.

+ **Play "Twenty Questions"**—to help your child learn how to ask meaningful questions.

+ **Get into the rhythm.** Recite nursery rhymes or poems together to help train your child's ear for the rhythm of words.

+ **Tickle each other's funny bone.** Make up tongue twisters or tell jokes and riddles together.

LITERATURE AND READING

Ever heard of a first-grader who doesn't love books? It's pretty rare. Six-year-olds, even those who can already read, love to be read to. Some listen intently, staring into space, while others follow the print with their eyes and pick out words or other features they recognize. They let us know they understand by remembering parts of a story, comparing something from a story to their own life, or noticing special patterns, rhymes, or picture clues in a book.

A few first-graders seem to learn to read without much teaching, but most are in the process of gaining necessary skills. Good readers use many approaches when learning to read: They use the pictures and the words they've just read to help them figure out the next bit of text; they use what they know about letters and sounds and about how our language is put together; they read ahead when they get stuck on a word to see if other words will help them figure out a troublesome one.

FROM SCHOOL TO HOME

Reading is a big focus of the first-grade classroom. Your child listens to and discusses stories every day. She may describe characters in a story or explain why she did or did not like a particular story. She also plays reading games or does "partner reading" with another child. And she may retell familiar stories through skits or puppet shows.

When you read to your six-year-old at home, she'll comment on a story or point out words as you read; then she'll probably ask to look at the book when you're done. She'll look at the pictures to help her read words on a page. And, as in school, she may put on plays or skits to retell favorite stories. She uses books to interact with a younger sibling or a friend by picking out a favorite book and reading it out loud.

"Now I know not to just read the story but also to talk to my child about what we read: 'Who's the character? Why did he do what he did?'"

It's Your Turn

Reading is crucial to your child's learning success. To nurture her lifelong love of reading:

+ **Keep her books handy.** Put them in a bookcase that your child can always get to; keep it well-stocked with books you've bought or checked out at the library.

+ **Create a reading routine.** If possible, plan to read to your child at a regular time–at bedtime, perhaps–every day. No matter what, read to her daily.

+ **Help her to read.** Encourage your child to read a few pages from a simple primary reader during your story time; listen to and help her as she does.

+ **...and to find the words.** Instead of telling your child what a word is, ask questions about it: "Is there something in the picture that can help you?"; "What does the word sound like at the beginning?"

+ **Talk about the tale.** Discuss what happens in the story during and after reading.

+ **...and ask questions about it:** "Which part was your favorite? Why? Was there anything in that story that reminded you of our family? Was there a part that made you sad [mad, afraid]?"

+ **Read about what she loves.** Encourage her to pick out books about her favorite subjects: insects, sports, buildings, outer space, animals, families doing things together.

+ **Get professional help.** Take your child to the library, and encourage her to ask the librarian to help her find books on topics she is interested in.

+ **Tune in to tape.** Find interesting story tapes for your child to enjoy.

+ **Read about her life.** Read stories to your child that feature events also happening in her life, such as a trip to the dentist, a pet dying, or best friends sharing something together.

+ **Read alone, together.** Have a few minutes of quiet time each day when you and your child each look at or read your own book. As you model your appreciation of solo reading, you'll encourage your child's independent enjoyment of books.

WRITING AND SPELLING

Most first-graders have discovered the power of written words and are eager to try writing. At first, they write single words or short phrases, such as a caption for a drawing or a sign for a door. As their confidence grows, they begin to write simple stories, such as, "This is a house and a dog." Soon simple plots unfold, such as, "The dog is barking. It wants a bone."

Six-year-olds begin to notice that certain features of writing are standard practice: Capital letters are used only in special places; there are "grown-up" ways to spell words. If they feel their spelling must be perfect, they will write only those words they can spell perfectly. This means their writing won't be interesting or fun. That's why it's better to delay an emphasis on spelling lists and conventional writing rules until they have realized the joy of writing down their thoughts.

FROM SCHOOL TO HOME

Just as your child has many opportunities to read in his classroom, so does he write a variety of things every day: "morning messages" on the chalk board, notes to friends in other classes, stories, science observations, posters. He now uses periods at the ends of sentences, knows how to make upper- and lower-case letters, writes beginnings and endings to stories, and rewrites and revises his work. He also sounds out words when writing. He may keep a list of common "words I need for writing" in a journal or writing folder. And he shares his writing with the rest of the class and listens to classmates' responses.

When your six-year-old eats the last piece of bread in the house, he'll add *bread* to the shopping list. Or he may copy the word *bread*, as well as other words he doesn't yet know how to spell, from books, signs, and labels. You'll see him write both capital and lower-case letters, although he may not be sure which to use when. He may draw a picture of a family outing and label each person or write a sentence about the outing. And he's likely to make his own picture book by drawing and writing on a sheet of paper he folds in half.

IT's YOUR TURN

To help him do the write stuff:

- ✦ **Create a writing center.** Have a special place where writing and art materials are always available for your child.

- ✦ **Make him a scribe.** Ask your child to do small writing tasks for you: "Will you please write a note to remind me to call your teacher?"

- ✦ **Let him put it in a book.** Encourage your child to make books for fun, for gifts, or as reminders of special occasions.

- ✦ **Help him get it down.** It's fine to do some of the writing of a story with your child if the writing is difficult for him. What's important is that he wants to and tries to tell his story.

- ✦ **Query his tales.** Ask questions about the characters and actions in your child's stories: "What kind of a person is that woman in your picture?"; "Where are those two boys going?"; "What will happen next?"

- ✦ **Note the form.** Point out features of standard writing, such as periods, question marks, and upper- and lower-case letters, as you read with your child.

- ✦ **Hear his words.** Be an appreciative audience for your child's writing.

- ✦ **Have him write his thanks.** When your child receives gifts from friends or relatives, encourage him to write brief thank-you letters.

- ✦ **Use signs.** Help your child make some signs for your house, such as "This is _____'s room" or "The bathroom."

- ✦ **Let him leave special notes.** Help your child write a happy message for Mom, Dad, or a sibling to put under a dinner plate or into a briefcase or lunch bag.

- ✦ **Clap it out together.** Help your child hear syllables or parts of words by clapping for each syllable as he says the word: "How many parts does *puppy* have? Let's clap and find out. *Pup-py.* That's right, two parts! What sounds do you hear in each part?"

- ✦ **Make a word book.** Help your child keep a personal dictionary of words he writes often.

- ✦ **Don't spell it out—too much.** Be relaxed about your child's spelling; let him take risks when he's trying to spell new words.

- ✦ **Give the gift of words.** Let your child write and illustrate a story, make a cover, and bind it with staples or yarn into book form. He could even put in an "About the author" section. Parents and grandparents love to receive books written by their favorite six-year-old.

CHAPTER 4

Mathematical Thinking

✦

Six-year-olds are learning their arithmetic facts: 6 + 4 = 10; 12 - 6 = 6. But mathematical thinking involves much more than just learning number facts and arithmetic sums. Mathematical thinking is about seeing patterns and relationships, figuring out more than one way to solve a problem, and discovering different systems for matching, combining, or dividing numbers. Children acquire mathematical skills and knowledge by manipulating a variety of physical objects, looking for patterns, judging the size of numbers, and solving problems creatively. Their progress can be seen in these four areas:

Patterns and relationships

Numbers and their use

Geometry, spatial relations, and measurement

Probability and statistics

PATTERNS AND RELATIONSHIPS

A large part of the mathematical thinking your child will do from now through high school—and beyond—has to do with understanding patterns and relationships. Six-year-olds know what patterns are and can make them with sounds, colors, shapes, and objects. They copy patterns, continue patterns, and create new patterns. They also notice patterns in the world around them.

First-graders are beginning to see and explain how groups of objects are related. They can compare the size of groups: "There are more clothespins on the line than there are in the bag." They can put items into a planned sequence, for example, arranging their books on a shelf from smallest to largest. They can also sort items into different categories by color, shape, size, and so on, and can explain the rules they use for sorting: "I put all the dark-colored ones here and all the light-colored ones over there."

FROM SCHOOL TO HOME

Patterns and relationships play a large part in your first-grader's school experience. She builds designs with pattern blocks, then makes pictures of the designs and uses words to describe them. She sorts collections of objects, describes the rule she used to sort them, and draws pictures of her work. She also sorts during daily tasks, such as arranging Lego pieces or colors of markers or organizing things during clean-up time. Many of her school projects will involve sorting. In social studies, she may have to go through a collection of pictures of buildings and sort them into groups of city buildings, town buildings, and country buildings. And, of course, your child puts together puzzles and can explain how she chooses pieces to fit.

While walking in your neighborhood, your six-year-old will notice the pattern of house numbers on a street and will predict the number of the next house, saying, "It's like skip-counting; you just skip a number." She may make up a simple dance pattern—two hops and a spin repeated over and over—and teach it to you. As you read together, she may notice a pattern of words in a story and predict when those words will appear again. Watch as your child sorts marbles or crayons and explains her sorting rule or arranges a collection of shells from smallest to largest.

It's Your Turn

To promote your child's pattern and sorting perceptions:

+ **Give her some duties—of a sort.** Have your child do household sorting tasks: laundry, groceries, coins.

+ **Go on road hunts.** Make up traveling games that involve looking for patterns along the roadside, such as on signs, in house designs, or in yard plantings.

+ **Play a sorting game:** One of you sorts objects, such as buttons or bottle caps, and the other one tries to guess the sorting rule.

+ **Point out patterns**—as you ride or walk around: "Look at that fence. The slats go plain, fancy, plain, fancy."

+ **Pattern numbers.** Create number sequences for your child to extend: for example, 2, 4, 8, 4, 2, 4, 8, 4, and so on.

+ **Say "buzz."** Pick a number between 1 and 10—for example, 5. Then start counting—1, 2, 3, etc.—taking turns saying the numbers. Every time one of you comes to a number with a 5 in it (5, 15, 25, 35), that person says "buzz" instead of the number.

+ **Frame her art.** Help your child draw pattern borders around drawings and paintings.

+ **Clap!** Create a clapping pattern (two claps and a space; three claps and a space; two claps and a space) and have your child imitate it; then have your child create a clapping pattern for you to imitate.

+ **Try some fancy footwork.** Make up a pattern with steps and jumps, and have your child imitate it (2 quick steps, jump, 2 quick steps, jump).

+ **Read by topic.** Help your child arrange her books on the shelf by topics: for example, books about animals here, books about families there, adventure stories over here.

NUMBERS AND THEIR USE

First-graders know a lot about numbers! They know that a number is more than just a word, it is a quantity: "Four" means there are 4 of something. They can count by memory up to fairly high numbers, often to 100 and beyond. They can count by 2s, 5s, and 10s. They can estimate or guess quantities with increasing accuracy, because they have a good idea of how much 20 really is and that 50 is a lot more than 20.

Children this age also know that they can join two groups of objects together—in other words, they can add. They also know that they can take some objects away from a group and make it smaller—subtraction. They need a lot of experience using actual objects to figure out addition or subtraction problems. Gradually, they start to work written problems and memorize addition and subtraction facts. First-graders are learning about place value, that 16 means one 10 and six 1s. This helps them learn to add and subtract large numbers: For example, to add 12 and 23, they add 10 and 20 to get 30 and 2 and 3 to get 5, which is 35.

FROM SCHOOL TO HOME

Count on it. Your six-year-old counts, reads, writes, adds, and subtracts numbers every day in school. For example, he reads a number and counts out objects equal to that number. He guesses, or estimates, the number of M&Ms or marbles in a large jar and then writes down the number. He may play a numbers game, in which he adds up the dots on two dice, or makes up, solves, and explains word problems, such as, "How many wheels are on six bikes?" In class he demonstrates a large number by counting out dimes and pennies or 10s and 1s rods. And he might use tally marks to keep track of the number of school days, grouping them by five.

Your six-year-old's number skills will show up at home, too. He's eager to count larger and larger numbers of objects. He'll make guesses about how many cookies are in a package, or how much the dog weighs. You may notice him add and subtract to figure out how many spaces to move on a board game. He'll also look forward to a birthday party or a visit with a relative by counting the number of days until the event and marking them off on a calendar.

It's Your Turn

To keep your child on the math track:

✦ **Let him keep score.** Play games that use numbers and ask your child to add up the points.

✦ **Have him "guesstimate":** "How many cars do you think are in this parking lot?" "How many people are waiting in line ahead of us?"

✦ **Throw math word questions at him:** "If you grew six more fingers, how many would you have all together? How did you figure that out?"

✦ **...and have him do the same to you.** Challenge your child to make up word problems for *you* to solve.

✦ **Create counting routines.** Practice counting dimes and pennies with your child; ask him to find a short cut for counting all the pennies.

✦ **Play with play money.** Let your child make pretend money and play "store," using empty food containers, old clothes, or other household objects.

✦ **Challenge his shopping savvy.** For example, ask your child to figure out how much two cans of soup will cost.

✦ **Eat by the numbers.** Have your child count out the right number of cookies for dessert so that everyone gets three.

✦ **Do a "digit-al" car trip:** Look for the numbers 1 through 100 on signs and license plates, or have your child tally how many cows, dogs, and cats (or trucks, vans, and trailers) he sees.

✦ **Count by machine.** Teach your child simple tasks on a calculator.

✦ **Compute on a computer.** Teach your child to play math games on a computer, such as those you find for free on the Web.

✦ **Give him the answer.** Tell your child a number (6, for example) and ask him to think of problems that have that number as the answer (3 + 3; 2 + 4; 7 − 1; 12 − 6).

✦ **Query his answer.** Ask your child how he solved a word problem that had numbers in it: "How did you figure that out?"; "Can you draw me a picture to show me how you did that?"

GEOMETRY, SPATIAL RELATIONS, AND MEASUREMENT

Young children are fascinated by shapes and how they can be organized and positioned in space. First-graders can describe shapes, talk about what makes them similar and different, play games with them, create designs, and so on. They make structures using pattern blocks, tangrams (shapes that make up other shapes), geoboards (surfaces that have pins on which rubber bands can be stretched into different shapes), and counting rods (wooden pieces that represent different unit amounts) that are balanced and symmetrical.

Another aspect of mathematical thinking is measurement. First-graders continue to use non-standard units, such as arms or strips of paper, to figure out length. But they also begin to see that standard measuring units are important, because arms can be different lengths. Measuring time (hours, days, months) is very challenging. Children benefit from lots of talk about schedules and references to the clock when thinking about how much time will pass until something specific occurs. For example, "There are three school weekends before your birthday," or, "Your dentist appointment is at one o'clock—right after lunch and recess at school."

FROM SCHOOL TO HOME

The first-grade classroom is full of shapes, relationships, and measurements. Your child makes designs with shape blocks or paper shapes. She goes on outdoor "shape treasure hunts." She can solve shape problems with pattern blocks by finding more than one way to make a shape. She creates designs with rubber bands on peg boards or geoboards and then may copy the patterns on paper. She measures ingredients for a cooking project with standard measuring cups and spoons. She may find out how many paper clips tall her friend is.

Outside of school you'll see your child find different shapes in the world around her: "Did you see that car with the hexagon on the front of it?" At home she'll make things with folded paper and then describe what she's done: "You start with a square and then fold it in half so you can see two triangles." She may draw pictures of her home, school, or room that show objects in the right places relative to other objects. She now knows the words for measuring tools: "Let's look at the thermometer to find out if I need a heavy jacket." And she'll begin using words for standard measurement units: "How many miles is it to Grandma's house?"

IT'S YOUR TURN

Watch things shape up and weigh in for your child as you:

+ **Play shape games.** Have bingo cards that have shapes to match rather than numbers, as well as puzzles and design blocks on hand to enjoy with your child.

+ **Play "guess the shape":** "I'm thinking of a shape. You ask me questions about it until you can guess what it is."

+ **Draw shapely things.** Teach your child to draw objects by naming the shapes they are made of: "One way to draw a house is to start with a triangle for the roof and attach a square for the bottom part."

+ **...and cut them out, too.** Together, make paper snowflakes or other shapes by folding a square or round piece of paper and cutting out small shapes on the folded edges.

+ **Give her a space quiz.** Challenge your child to figure out how much space things take up: "Do you think your clothes will fit into this bag?"; "Can you build a barn that will hold all of your animals?"; "What size box will you need for your collection of markers?"

+ **Have her run a verbal treasure hunt.** Play games that require word directions to find things. For example, let your child hide something and then sit on her hands and direct you to it, using only words.

+ **Discuss puzzle strategy.** As you and your child work puzzles together, talk about the ways you select pieces, such as matching colors, joining shapes with prongs, and so on.

+ **Teach her to measure.** Have some common measuring tools (scale, tape measure, thermometer, measuring cups, kitchen timer) around your home and help your child use them.

+ **Then let her measure up.** Involve your child in household measurement tasks—measuring wood for a construction project, laying out a garden plot, weighing a pet, measuring ingredients for a recipe and then timing the baking.

+ **Assign her regular tasks**—such as reporting the morning temperature each day and measuring out the pet's food.

+ **Let her keep dates.** Help your child keep a monthly calendar, marking both routine and special events.

+ **Chart her changes.** Measure and weigh your child once a month and keep a chart of her growth.

PROBABILITY AND STATISTICS

Probability and statistics may sound complicated, but for first-graders it simply means learning how to collect and display information. Six-year-olds enjoy collecting information (game scores, daily temperatures, the number of shells in their collection), conducting surveys (what kind of ice cream people like best, which sports people play), and showing results in different ways (tallies, lists, charts, and graphs).

FROM SCHOOL TO HOME

In school your child deals with statistics when he surveys the class, makes a chart or a graph to show the results, and then draws some conclusions. He may create graphs using real objects: For example, a graph titled "How we get to school" displays a stack of green blocks to show the number of bus riders, red blocks to show car riders, and yellow blocks to show walkers. He may make a graph that shows which types of buildings students live in and use it to answer questions: "How many children live in apartments? How many children live in houses? Do more children live in houses or apartments? How many more?" Your first-grader will also keep track of and use mathematical information. For example, he'll figure out how many school days have passed by using tally marks and then count by 5s to find the total number of marks that have been made.

At home you will notice your child's interest in probability and statistics grow. He may create charts or graphs to display information about a collection of sports cards or miniature animals. He may keep tally or number scores in games he plays with friends. He may create a survey or questionnaire sheet to find out which kind of juice or soda people would like at a family get-together. He'll be interested in graphing the number of days that are left before a school vacation.

"I never realized before that jobs around the house, like helping match socks, are not just jobs. You're talking about size and color, about counting, making pairs, and dividing in half. It's very math oriented."

IT'S YOUR TURN

To nurture your young statistician:

+ **Have him keep track.** Help your child collect information and organize it on a graph: types of coins in the piggy bank, game scores, family food preferences, television-watching time.

+ **Chart a family plan.** Post information your child needs: weekly schedules of family members, household chores, appointments with the doctor.

+ **...and a birthday schedule.** Keep a chart showing in which months family members' birthdays fall.

+ **Let him see his successes.** Help your child keep a chart of how often he does his chores or homework without being reminded.

+ **Help him manage his money.** Have your child keep a record of how he spends his allowance or how much money he earns doing small jobs.

+ **Watch plants grow.** After planting a garden or potting a bulb, help your child graph the ongoing growth progress.

+ **Tally his guesses.** For example, before starting out in the car to go to the store, guess with your child how many cars you will pass based on the number of streets and the traffic density; then keep a tally sheet to check out your estimates.

+ **Roll that die!** Help your child make a chart showing which number comes up each time he rolls a die. Find out which number comes up most often in 25 rolls of the die. Playing with dice is a fun way to learn for six-year-olds.

+ **Spot sports stats.** Follow the statistics—wins and losses, number of points scored, how fast runners run—of your child's favorite athletes or sports team.

+ **Track the weather.** Help your child learn to look at newspaper weather charts and graphs and figure out what the weather is like in other parts of the country.

CHAPTER 5

Scientific Thinking

✦

Learning science is more than just learning facts. Young students of science learn ways of discovering and thinking about their world. They begin to understand that scientists are the detectives of the world around them. They also realize that at any age they, too, can be science detectives. Thinking and acting like a scientist means:

**Observing, investigating,
and questioning**

**Predicting, explaining, and
forming conclusions**

OBSERVING, INVESTIGATING, AND QUESTIONING

First-graders are naturally curious. They are good observers who look hard at things and notice details by using more than just their eyes as they listen with growing awareness to sounds, identify a variety of odors, and use their fingers to explore surfaces, textures, and density of materials. They are learning that certain instruments can help them in their observations, such as a magnifying glass, binoculars, a tape recorder, a scale, and a thermometer.

As they examine and explore, six-year-olds ask many questions that are increasingly focused and detailed. They want to know how things work, where things come from, what will happen next, and so on. To search for answers, they look in books for information, ask someone who might know, and construct simple experiments. They are learning new ways to keep track of what they learn—graphs, charts, log books, lists, detailed drawings.

FROM SCHOOL TO HOME

Your child's classroom is an exploration zone with interesting things to observe, scientific tools to use, and a ready audience to inform. She may observe natural objects, such as stones, leaves, or shells, describe them, and sort them into categories based on their shape, texture, size, or color. She will use a magnifying lens to see an insect more closely, a scale to weigh rock specimens precisely, or a ruler to measure the growth of plants more exactly. As she gathers information, she will record it in careful drawings, charts, and graphs. Your young scientist may also become involved in a science investigation that lasts several days and will then report her discoveries to her classmates.

While out and about, your six-year-old will show interest in outdoor sounds, strong smells, the feel of certain stones, or the details of an insect's body. She'll borrow a magnifying glass to look at a bug or a leaf. She may find seeds outdoors and plant them to see what grows. At home she'll watch steam rise from a pot on the stove and ask questions about fog, clouds, and rain. You'll see her grow interested in a new pet or hobby and try to learn more about it. Before she gets ready for school, your child might check the thermometer before choosing which clothes to wear.

IT'S YOUR TURN

To nurture your child's budding curiosity:

+ **Query her senses.** Ask your child about what she's noticed: "Did you see anything interesting on your way to school today?"; "Can you think of something else that smells like that?"; "What do you think made that sound?"

+ **Train her nose.** Play "name that smell" by putting small amounts of strong-smelling foods (vinegar, peanut butter, cinnamon, etc.) in small jars and having your child smell each one to learn their special odors. Then see if she can name each smell wearing a blindfold.

+ **Incite her curiosity.** Ask exploratory questions: "How could we find out?"; "What would happen if...?"

+ **Play "Twenty Questions."** Think of an object, animal, or person and give your child 20 questions to try to figure out the subject you have in mind.

+ **Give her the tools.** Have handy and teach your child to use a magnifying glass, binoculars, thermometer, and scale.

+ **Let her loose in the "lab."** Help your child set up simple tests or experiments so she can answer some of her own questions: "How does my skin look under a magnifying glass?"; "Do plants grow in the dark?"

+ **Nurture her natural instincts:** Ask questions about your child's scientific interests; take her to the library to do research; set up a field trip to help her find new items for a collection.

+ **Let her take the long view.** Help your child make a mock telescope with paper-towel tubes and encourage her to look at things that are far away.

+ **Play "guess what I see."** Pick out an object and give clues until your child can figure out what you are describing; take turns being the describer and the guesser.

+ **Plant a "garbage garden."** Place carrot tops, potatoes, avocado pits, or pineapple tops in water in front of a window and watch them grow.

+ **Make leaf rubbings.** Put a leaf under tissue paper and rub over it gently with a crayon to raise the pattern; help your child notice the varying patterns of different leaves and learn what kind of trees they come from.

PREDICTING, EXPLAINING, AND FORMING CONCLUSIONS

First-graders like to answer the questions "Why do you think this happened?" and "What do you think will happen next?" However, their answers are not always based on facts. Six-year-olds are becoming increasingly skilled at making logical predictions, but they don't quite have the experience to be able to give correct explanations or conclusions all the time. As young scientists, they need to use their observations to try to explain *why* things happen. Making reasonable explanations and sharing these explanations with others by talking, drawing, and writing are important parts of the scientific-thinking process.

FROM SCHOOL TO HOME

In school your first-grader makes predictions based on his investigations: He takes notes, draws pictures, asks questions, and forms conclusions as he watches a caterpillar form a chrysalis and become a butterfly. He also uses past experience to make predictions about new things: "The butterfly took about a week to come out of the chrysalis, but I think the chickens will take longer to hatch because they are bigger." He predicts what kinds of things will float and what will sink and then explains his guesses: Your child also records his findings. He may, for example, test different growing conditions for plants by varying the light, water, and soil and keep track of what he finds out in a science log; or he'll experiment with balls made from different materials to find out which ones bounce highest, then he'll make a graph to show the results.

All kinds of scientific processes around the house will inspire your six-year-old. He may watch birds feeding outside and keep track of which seeds they like; then he might explain how birds use their beaks to crack the shells of the seeds. Perhaps he'll watch an electrician at work, ask some questions, and then tell a friend about what he learned. Your child might draw a picture of a garden, which shows that plants have different heights, colors, and shapes; next, he might write the names of some of the plants and predict which ones will stay in bloom all summer long and which will have flowers for only a short time. After a rain shower, you may see him look for a rainbow, first predicting where it will appear and then asking how rainbows happen.

It's Your Turn

To keep his good guesses coming:

✦ **Coax his conclusions.** Ask questions to help your child think of explanations: "Why do you think this happened?"; "Why did you decide to do it this way?"; "How would you describe that plant to someone who couldn't see it?"

✦ **Question his conclusions:** "How do you know the train will come in on that track?"; "How did you know what would happen when you put that in water?"

✦ **Recall memories.** Remind your child of past experiences that might help him explain a new situation: "Do you remember the fish you caught last summer? What happened to its scales?"; "Do you remember when we left the ice cream on the counter? What do you think happened to these ice cubes?"

✦ **Give him the words.** Teach your child new words that will help him talk and write about what he sees: For example, a good time to teach the word *camouflage* is when your excited child talks about finding a green snake in the grass and how hard it was to see it.

✦ **Listen!** Show interest and curiosity in your child's scientific explanations and conclusions.

✦ **Play "mini-mysteries."** Make up a mysterious situation and ask your child to explain it: "The girl came into the kitchen. The refrigerator door was open, but nothing was missing. There were footprints leading out the door. Can you explain what happened?"

✦ **Explore on-screen science.** Watch science or nature programs on television and discuss how the scientists you see make their discoveries.

✦ **Write a scientific journal:** Make a book called *This Is What I Know and This Is How I Know It*, and help your child write about one new discovery each week.

✦ **Praise his predictions.** It takes courage to make them. So applaud his efforts, even when they are not accurate.

✦ **Spark his scientific imagination.** Describe situations and end with "What happens next?": "Shannon and Lyle are playing on the playground, and it starts to rain; what happens next?"; "The butcher gives the dog a bone; what happens next?"

✦ **Talk about the weather:** Listen to weather predictions on television or radio, and talk about how weather forecasters know what tomorrow will bring.

CHAPTER 6

Social Studies

✦

For children, social studies involves learning how to understand our society and culture. First-graders are ready to expand their thinking about likenesses and differences among people and cultures, to look beyond their personal experience at the characteristics of groups of people, and to explore our dependence on each others' skills and resources. Six-year-olds are beginning to think about the meaning of rules, why we have them, and what would happen without them. Children begin their study of these concepts in two areas:

People and how they live their lives

How the past, the land, and people affect one another

PEOPLE AND HOW THEY LIVE THEIR LIVES

First-graders are becoming aware of human similarities and differences, of the many ways people depend on one another, and of what it takes for people to live together peacefully. They know we all need to eat, live somewhere, and have clothes to wear. They are just beginning to understand how many different kinds of workers it takes to provide these things. In addition, they are fascinated with the tools and machines that help make people's lives easier and safer.

Children this age are learning that all people belong to a variety of groups and that these groups affect how we live. They have a basic understanding that groups need rules and leaders so that things are fair for everyone. Six-year-olds are familiar with the rules at school and realize that they might be different from rules at home. They are beginning to think about rules and leaders in communities and in government. They are also aware of how leaders function in groups and are able to identify the qualities that make good leaders.

FROM SCHOOL TO HOME

In school your first-grader gains awareness of the world of people in many ways. The people she draws, paints, or creates as puppets begin to differ from one another; they have different skin colors, vary in size, wear a variety of clothing. She may study different buildings people live in and make models for towns or cities. Chances are that she'll learn a lot about jobs people have. There will be discussions about jobs described in books, opportunities to listen to visitors talk about their jobs, and she may even think up questions and interview someone about the work she or he does. She'll practice what she learns by working on a group project in which everybody has different jobs. She'll learn how democratic communities work as she takes part in class meetings to discuss rules, vote on issues, or talk over social problems that arise.

Your child may come home and draw pictures of, discuss, and ask questions about people of different ages, genders, or races. She'll ask where things come from: "Who grew this? Who made that?" She'll express her curiosity about various jobs and talk about what she'd like to do when she grows up. Her new-found appreciation of rules may inspire her to insist that rules in games be followed to the letter.

IT'S YOUR TURN

To help her appreciate the people in her world:

+ **Broaden her book horizons.** Read books about people who are different from you and discuss them with your child.

+ **Voice respect for variety.** Help your child appreciate human differences—and how they are a part of human strength—so she is not afraid of people who are different from her.

+ **Tap into international tunes.** Listen to music from many parts of the world and discuss its characteristics and variety with your child.

+ **Make a people collage together.** Cut out pictures of different kinds of people from magazines; talk about the people as you turn the cut-outs into a collage of diversity.

+ **Examine your images.** Look in a mirror with your child and list all the ways you and she are the same and different.

+ **Say *buenos dias, bonjour,* or *ni hao*!** Learn how to say a few words in other languages. (These words are Spanish, French, and Mandarin Chinese for *hello*.)

+ **Take her to work.** Show your child what you do and what tools, machines, and equipment you use.

+ **Read about community spirit.** As you read books together, look for examples of how people in families, communities, and jobs work together to get things done.

+ **Engage in occupational play.** Give your child props—a hard hat, a food-server's apron, a stethoscope, blueprint paper—and help her pretend to be different kinds of workers.

+ **Make a "My Community Book":** In it, draw pictures of some of the people who help your community run smoothly.

+ **Have her express thanks.** Help your child write a thank-you note to a community person or worker who has been helpful, such as a teacher, scout leader, coach, dentist, or store clerk.

+ **Discuss rules**—why we need rules and laws and what life would be like without them. For example, ask what it would be like if we didn't have traffic laws.

+ **Sketch out the rules.** Make a poster of family rules and let your child draw pictures to illustrate each one.

+ **Play rule games**—such as "Simon Says" or "Follow the Leader"—so your child can know how it feels to sometimes be the leader and sometimes the follower.

HOW THE PAST, THE LAND, AND PEOPLE AFFECT ONE ANOTHER

For first-graders, learning about the past is fascinating and meaningful when they learn about their own family's history—where their parents and grandparents lived as children, what their homes, schools, and places of worship were like, how they cooked their meals, what jobs they did. Figuring out what is the same and what is different between their own lives and the childhood lives of their parents and grandparents helps six-year-olds see the threads of history. Children this age can also understand the way people have affected the environment, both in the past and in the present. They can begin to see how human activities, such as farming, building dams and bridges, laying down roads, creating cities, putting up factories, and making dumps, have both good and bad effects on the land. When history and geography come alive, first-graders pay attention!

FROM SCHOOL TO HOME

First-grade teachers help children develop historical perspective by helping them research the past. Your child and his classmates might interview older people about what school was like, collect artifacts from the "olden days," and put on a skit, incorporating what they learned. The teacher may collect old photographs of the community where you live so your child can make timelines and maps showing how things used to be. The first-grade geographers may paint murals of different landscapes and use them for the scenery behind skits that show how people live and work in different places. Your six-year-old will be an enthusiastic participant in the school's recycling program. And he will learn that maps are a special kind of picture that tells about the land. He'll also try making maps himself.

At home your child will ask questions about when you were a child. He may also look at old family photographs and discuss the funny clothes or how different the cars were then. To gain a sense of proximity to the world, he'll ask for help to draw a map of his room or of the walk to school. He may point out special aspects of the area in which he lives: "I'm glad we live near the mountains so we can go hiking," or, "We live in the city so there are lots of things to visit." As in school, he'll be concerned with his environment and may remind family members to recycle a bottle or newspaper instead of throwing it in the trash.

It's Your Turn

You'll encourage his awareness of the past and present when you:

✦ **Let him shape his life.** Help your child make a scrapbook, photo album, or timeline of his life.

✦ **Read historical fiction**—children's books about the past, such as the Little House books by Laura Ingalls Wilder—and talk about similarities and differences between then and now.

✦ **Look back.** Go through photo albums and talk about the lives of older members of the family—your child's grandparents, great grandparents, and aunts and uncles.

✦ **Have him question his elders.** Suggest questions for your child to ask grandparents or other older people about their lives as children.

✦ **Go back.** Talk about what life was like when there was no electricity, cars, or television, and maybe even try living without one or two of these commodities for a day.

✦ **Seek out the past.** Visit historical museums to learn about life in the past (several short trips will be better than one long one).

✦ **Map out the route.** When you plan a trip, look at maps with your child and let him follow the trip's progress.

✦ **Make a map to the treasure.** Plan treasure hunts in which your child has to follow a simple map to find a surprise.

✦ **Make make-believe maps.** Together, draw maps of favorite or imaginary places.

✦ **Compare far-away places.** Read books with your child about different parts of the world and talk about, for example, the housing, the native trees and flowers, or the clothes the children might wear in each locale.

✦ **Let him get seasonal.** Ask your child to help you prepare for changing weather or seasons: Batten down for a hurricane or blizzard, put on storm windows or snow tires, maintain window fans, clean out gutters.

✦ **Encourage the environmentalist in him.** Involve your child in your family's efforts to improve the environment by recycling, picking up litter, planting a community garden.

CHAPTER 7

The Arts

✦

Drawing, painting, sculpting, drama, dance, and music are key ingredients of learning for young children. Children often have ideas and feelings that they can't express through talking or writing. The arts provide languages that even young children can easily use. In addition, these are languages that children can understand when other people use them. Two aspects of arts education are:

Artistic expression

Artistic appreciation

ARTISTIC EXPRESSION

First-graders' minds are full of ideas, experiences, and emotions. For many children this age, talking or writing about their ideas is difficult; expressing them through the arts is easier. When adults are present to appreciate their efforts, six-year-olds show what they learn and think about through drawing, painting, sculpting, singing, moving, or building. They express their creativity and imagination with crayons, markers, paints, clay, sounds, and movements. These media enable children to experiment freely and solve problems along the way.

FROM SCHOOL TO HOME

The first-grade classroom is a mecca for creative expression. Your six-year-old creates many kinds of art projects: collages, sculptures, drawings, paintings, sketches. She also uses different materials for building, such as Legos, blocks, straws, and boxes. She has the opportunity to put on skits and puppet shows about things she is learning. She sings, makes up songs, and plays musical instruments in class, and she moves or dances to many different kinds of music. Your child may combine several art forms, such as painting or dancing to music or making up words for a song to describe an adventure or a feeling.

Around the house your little artist uses odds and ends of creative "junk" to make designs, pictures, or sculptures. You'll see her create unusual and complex designs, such as buildings or creatures, using blocks or Legos. She may make a musical instrument, such as a kazoo by wrapping wax paper or tissue around a comb or a drum from a coffee can, and think up ways to make new sounds. She'll ask you to be the audience for a play she's made up about an event or an imaginary person. And she may use paper, markers, and scissors to make a menu for a pretend restaurant or tickets for a play she wants you to watch.

"These ideas are wonderful tools that carry normal daily life one step further, strengthening parent/child relationships."

It's Your Turn

To encourage your child's creativity:

✦ **Keep art supplies on hand**—both store-bought, such as crayons, markers, paints, clay, colored pencils, and pens, and recycled, such as Popsicle sticks, straws, tin foil, fabric scraps, yarn, Styrofoam, wallpaper samples, pieces of wood, and natural objects—so that your child always has the materials for creative expression.

✦ **Show her *your* inner Rembrandt.** Find space and time to create works of art with your child with finger paints, paper and paste, clay, or play dough.

✦ **Be her audience**—and enjoy her musical or dramatic productions.

✦ **Compliment her creative thinking.** Praise your child's creative use of materials and solutions to problems: "I never would have thought to use pieces of tinfoil for the roofs of the houses!"

✦ **Write lyrics together.** Make up new words to familiar tunes.

✦ **Indulge in creative freedom.** With your child, have fun with scribble art, make pinhole pictures, do fabric painting, create partner pictures.

✦ **Let one art form influence another.** Draw pictures with your child while listening to your favorite music.

✦ **Do the dance of life together.** Have fun making up movements that imitate animals, machines, the weather, birds, and so on.

✦ **Start from scratch.** Make homemade play dough together; then use it to make a house like yours, or a dog or a bird, or letters of the alphabet.

✦ **Put the icing on the cake.** Let your child decorate a cake or cupcakes with a tube of colored frosting.

✦ **Design letters.** With your child, create patterns and designs across the top or bottom of a letter to a relative.

✦ **Craft cards.** Make original greeting cards with your child using stars, glitter, markers, stickers, and pictures cut out of magazines.

ARTISTIC APPRECIATION

Although some first-graders are hesitant to act, sing, or dance themselves, they are able to view and show interest in the artistic endeavors of others, and think about what an artist, dancer, or composer is trying to communicate. They understand that the colors, shapes, sounds, and movements are an artist's way of speaking.

FROM SCHOOL TO HOME

At school your child can be an active art enthusiast. He responds positively to a classmate's artistic expressions during group time. He reacts to concerts or plays given by other students or outside performers by discussing, writing about, or drawing them. He has the opportunity to appreciate different kinds of music by listening during quiet time or at the listening center; he may even paint as he listens. Your six-year-old might write a letter of appreciation to a parent who came to class to demonstrate how to sculpt or play a musical instrument. Perhaps he'll focus on a particular children's book illustrator and talk about the artist's work.

At home you'll hear your first-grader sing songs he's learned at school and then say, for example, "Doesn't this song make you feel happy?" He may enjoy and talk about the artwork in a book, or compliment the artwork of a friend or sibling. He'll also respond appreciatively to a magician or artist performing in the park, mall, or street.

IT'S YOUR TURN

To encourage your young art enthusiast:

✦ **Museum-hop.** Go to museums for short visits, encouraging your child to talk with the museum staff about the collections.

✦ **See pictures at an exhibition.** Go to an art exhibit with your child, and talk about what he thinks a particular artist was thinking when painting the picture you are viewing. Also discuss the medium used by the painter and how it affects the mood of the scene.

✦ **Note those notes.** Stop and listen to a musician playing in the mall or on the street.

✦ **Admire the architecture.** Point out interesting buildings in the city, and talk with your child about how buildings are designed and built and how architects are artists.

✦ **Appreciate craftspeople.** Go to an arts-and-crafts fair to see different kinds of artists at work: potters, weavers, painters, wood carvers.

✦ **See a play.** Then talk with your child about what he liked and how he felt the actors portrayed the story.

✦ **Attend a concert.** Talk together about how the music created moods and feelings; ask your child if any stories came to mind as he listened to the orchestra.

✦ **See a film about a familiar topic.** Pick a movie or video about something you and your child have been reading about. After viewing it, discuss how the movie portrayed the subject in a way different from the book. Talk about how the author of the book might feel about the way the topic was adapted for film.

✦ **Appreciate puppetry.** Attend a puppet show at school or in the neighborhood; talk with your child about the story and how well the puppets were able to communicate it.

✦ **Enjoy the clowns.** Go to a circus or a parade and discuss with your child the skills needed and practiced by the various performers.

✦ **Research the arts.** At the library, ask for children's books about various well-known artists—painters, sculptors, musicians.

CHAPTER 8

Physical Development and Health

✦

Children's physical development and the health of their bodies are very important to their mental health and growth. Six-year-olds are gaining in their ability to move in ways that demonstrate control, balance, and coordination, all of which enhance their sense of well-being and competence. Six-year-olds need to develop their ability to use their hands for writing, artistic expression, and performing self-help skills. This is crucial to their sense of self and their ability to function with confidence. Developing healthy ways of taking care of themselves is also important in first grade. Physical development and health can be seen in three areas:

Large-muscle development

Small-muscle development

Personal health and safety

LARGE-MUSCLE DEVELOPMENT

First-graders are in the process of developing physical balance and control. They are working to coordinate several different kinds of movement at the same time. Always active, if not always graceful, they are learning how to move with increasing purpose and skill.

FROM SCHOOL TO HOME

At school your child has plenty of opportunities for movement. She plays games that require basic physical skills, such as running, hopping, and jumping, as well as throwing, catching, and kicking a ball. She is also mastering new skills, such as balancing on a beam, turning cartwheels, or standing on her head. With her peers she builds and uses obstacle courses, both indoors and outdoors. She is encouraged to move in different ways to music. And she performs physical chores in the classroom: putting chairs up, passing out materials, moving boxes of toys.

Watch your child at home as she carries plates of food or glasses of milk without spilling. You'll also see her run, skip, hop, jump, and climb with ease, strength, and speed. She can now jump rope and turn around in circles at the same time, or run and then kick a ball without stopping. Your six-year-old will swing a bat or a racket and hit a ball with increasing accuracy. And she'll impress you by trying tricks on her bicycle.

It's Your Turn

To keep your child on the move:

+ **Send her out and about.** Make sure your child gets plenty of active play—in the yard, at the park, in a gym. New research suggests that in school, children get only a few minutes per day of high-intensity activity, so lots of extra movement is important to your child's well-being.

+ **Get fit together.** Exercise with your child by jogging for short distances or throwing a Frisbee.

+ **...and stretch it out.** Do a few minutes of stretching exercises together every day.

+ **Encourage extracurricular action.** Help your child get involved with organized sports or recreation activities.

+ **Hold a Family Olympics.** Include running races, hopping and jumping contests, obstacle courses, and so on. Invite cousins, uncles, and aunts to join in!

+ **Track her speed.** Time your child to see how fast she can run a certain distance; keep track to see if she gets faster over time.

+ **Shoot hoops.** Set up a lower-than-standard-height basketball hoop and practice throwing baskets together, or simply throw a ball into a cardboard box.

+ **Hit the playground**—so your child can swing on the swings, climb on the jungle gym, slide down the slide, and run.

+ **Share outside chores.** Rake leaves, shovel snow, clear brush, and stack wood with your child.

+ **Shake a leg.** Dance with your child, creating dance routines as you listen to a variety of rhythms on the radio or a tape or CD.

SMALL-MUSCLE DEVELOPMENT

Six-year-olds are developing increasing strength and control in the small muscles of their hands, fingers, and wrists. They can coordinate their eyes and hands, which helps them handle small objects, use drawing and writing materials, and perform other small-motor tasks with greater precision. Their drawings and writing are becoming more detailed and accurate.

FROM SCHOOL TO HOME

First-graders have plenty to do with their hands in class. Your child uses hand tools and equipment, such as scissors, hole-punchers, staplers, typewriters, computer keyboards, and other drawing and writing tools. He engages in various projects that require small-muscle coordination: gluing small objects, stringing small beads, threading a needle and sewing, weaving, or carpentry. His handwriting improves as he, for example, writes in a journal for longer and longer periods of time. And he now puts together puzzles with smaller pieces.

You'll see your six-year-old use scissors, staplers, and other tools at home with increased control and strength. He'll write letters and draw figures more carefully and precisely; he'll strike single keys on a typewriter, computer, calculator, or piano. He is able to place small beads, blocks, or puzzle pieces just where he wants them. And he'll spend more time than ever with his blocks or Legos, building intricate structures. Of course he can now tie his shoelaces, button his shirt, and zip his jacket with ease.

IT'S YOUR TURN

You'll help his hands become more and more nimble when you:

+ **Keep supplies on hand.** Have fabric, yarn, beads, wire, clay, clothespins, paper clips, and recycled materials available for his hand-work projects.

+ **Applaud his skill.** Praise your child's efforts at creating projects, even when they aren't perfect.

+ **Give him some chores**—those that work his small muscles, such as setting the table, pouring milk, peeling vegetables, writing things on the shopping list, folding laundry.

+ **Hand him the pad and pencils.** Encourage your child to draw and write every day.

+ **Get crafty together.** Make cut-out figures, snowflakes, masks, and decorations with scissors, paper, and glue.

+ **Follow the fold.** Make folded paper objects together, such as hats, boats, origami figures, and paper boxes.

+ **String beads together.** Create a necklace or a decoration that could be attached to a belt.

+ **Show him the stitch.** Start a sewing, knitting, or weaving project with your child, in which you teach him how to perform the task and then you each work on your own piece of the project.

+ **Go in and out.** Weave strips of paper together to make place mats, or strips of cloth to make a quilt.

+ **Build Legos plus.** Create Lego structures with your child and suggest adding other materials—small blocks, paper or cardboard, small people figures, little cars—that will make the constructions more detailed.

+ **Play with your fingers together**—games that require small-motor skill, such as "Pick-Up-Sticks," marbles, or checkers.

+ **Play cards.** Try games such as "Concentration," in which he has to pick up and turn over cards, or "Kings in the Corner," in which he must move layers of cards from one place to another.

+ **Work trickier puzzles.** Provide more complicated puzzles that have smaller pieces than he is accustomed to, and together assemble a puzzle over several days or weeks.

+ **Work with tools.** Let your child participate in carpentry tasks you need to do, showing him how to use the tools safely and skillfully. Then help him build something he'd like, such as a simple bird feeder to put outside your window.

PERSONAL HEALTH AND SAFETY

Children this age are starting to understand that their behavior affects their health and safety. They know basic cleanliness and health habits, such as washing their hands, covering their mouth when coughing, eating healthy food, and getting rest. They may need reminders, however, to do these things regularly.

FROM SCHOOL TO HOME

In class your child is learning about parts of the human body and the things that make the body work well. This means, for one thing, that she takes part in a classroom exercise program. She also learns to identify nutritious foods and make healthy snacks. And of course she washes her hands before eating a snack or lunch. She may also perform simple first-aid procedures, such as cleaning and covering wounds and putting ice on bruises. She takes part in safety exercises, such as fire drills and bus evacuations. Aware of those around her, she picks up materials and cleans up messes so others will be safe.

Health and hygiene are becoming second nature at home. Your six-year-old washes her hands, combs her hair, and brushes her teeth with little help and few reminders. She also knows to get a tissue to wipe her runny nose. Don't be surprised when she tells others why they should drink milk, eat fruit, get exercise, or stop smoking. She'll show you that she can take care of herself, too: She'll know to wear a sweater and raincoat on a cold, wet day and to look both ways before crossing a street.

"These examples are great, because they show that you can give children responsibility while still expressing love and affection."

It's Your Turn

To help her take care of herself:

+ **Offer a little extra encouragement.** Give your child gentle reminders to cover her mouth when she coughs or sneezes and throw her soiled tissues in the wastebasket.

+ **Give her the thumbs-up.** Praise your child when she remembers health and safety behaviors on her own.

+ **Stay healthy and safe yourself.** Model good habits and practices as an example for your child, such as washing your hands before cooking, and buckling your seat belt when in a car.

+ **Focus on her "pearly whites."** Help her remember to brush her teeth after meals and at bed time.

+ **Raise a smart chef.** Let your child help you plan healthy meals as you talk with her about including items from each food group.

+ **Have family fire drills.**

+ **Let her monitor the detector.** Have your child help you change the batteries in the smoke detector.

+ **Do some pre–driver's ed.** Model and talk about safe driving habits when you are in the car, such as watching for other cars and looking out for children playing near the road.

+ **Make family health and safety rules.** Decide together on important rules and post them on a wall or the refrigerator door. For example: Wash hands after using the toilet; Wash hands before eating meals, handling food, or setting the table; Always buckle your seat belt in the car; Always wear a helmet when riding your bike.

+ **Let her be the leader.** Let your child tell you when it is safe to cross the street, where to stand on the steps of the escalator, or what to do when approaching a strange dog.

Winning Ways to Learn
for 7-Year-Olds

CHAPTER 9

Personal and Social Development

✦

Personal and social development continues to be a vital component of children's learning in second grade. Self-confidence is important to children's ability to learn. Among other things, confident children are willing to take risks and to fail—important aspects of learning.

Children's self-image and social skills shape how they interact with adults and other children. Getting along well is important in making school a place where children want to be and where they can learn to enjoy learning. Children's growth in this area is viewed through their:

Self-concept and self-control

Approach to learning

Interactions with others

SELF-CONCEPT AND SELF-CONTROL

Parents of seven-year-olds know that many children this age experience a dip in confidence. At age five and six, they were adventurous—experimenting with lots of new skills and ideas. Now, they are beginning to worry about perfecting those skills. With extra encouragement, however, they gradually become more independent and sure of their actions and decisions. Second-graders like to be in control; they rely on predictability. They are more likely to follow rules when they understand the reasons for them and when they have helped to set them. After receiving clear instructions, they handle materials carefully, needing only occasional reminders to be responsible. Changes in routine, such as a schedule shift or an unexpected visitor, may make second-graders feel insecure. Supportive adults help seven-year-olds reach new levels of self-reliance and self-assurance, which have a direct effect on their ability to learn.

From School to Home

There are many opportunities in the second-grade classroom for your child to grow in confidence, competence, and ease. He has learned to follow classroom rules and may remind others to do the same. He knows he can ask for help when he needs it or politely turn it down when he doesn't. He can find the materials he needs and return them when he is finished with them. He now chooses activities in which he is really interested, despite peer pressure to participate in other activities. And he seeks out work partners who share his interest in particular topics, such as animals, sports, or space travel.

At home your child mirrors what he practices in school. You'll find that he takes more responsibility for his belongings and needs. He uses his toys, books, and play equipment with more care and puts them away when he is finished using them. He may even volunteer to do an extra job around the house. His increasing confidence reveals itself when, for instance, he asks to ride his bike or walk a little farther away from home. For his own sense of comfort, he'll ask you to explain the reason for certain family rules and want to talk about possible changes in those rules.

It's Your Turn

To strengthen your seven-year-old's sense of self:

✦ **Ask and answer.** Encourage your child to think for himself by asking questions that motivate his response—"What happens if...?"; "How did you feel when...?"; "What do you think that means?" and so on. In turn, explain things in a way that challenges him to question you.

✦ **Feed him knowledge.** Help your child grow more capable by teaching him new skills, information, and words relating to things that interest both of you.

✦ **Encourage his independence.** Suggest activities that allow him to be safely self-reliant: walking the dog, using the telephone, biking to a nearby friend's house, running an errand.

✦ **Get his input.** When you involve your child in some family decision-making—what to have for dinner, what to do during vacation—you are letting him know his opinions matter.

✦ **...and give him useful tasks to do.** Help your child learn to be more responsible by giving him meaningful household chores: taking out the trash, watering plants, washing dishes, feeding pets.

✦ **Applaud his can-do attitude.** Praise your child's efforts to be independent and take charge of things: "You did a good job packing up your backpack for school!"

✦ **Show your joy**—when you talk and play with your child.

✦ **Ask for your child's help.** Let him assist you, for example, in preparing meals: He can chop vegetables, make a salad, stir the soup, prepare the batter for pancakes.

✦ **Give him some power.** Ask your child to help create family rules, and help him write them on a sign to put in a special place.

✦ **Compliment his cool.** Praise your child when he follows the rules or shows self-control.

✦ **Calmly ask for accountability.** Enforce family rules consistently; use reasonable consequences rather than severe punishment. For example, when he forgets to put away his coat, tell him he has to take care of it before he can watch television or use the computer.

✦ **Remind him to *think* before he *does*.** Ask your child to remember how to use materials and equipment properly before he takes them out and works with them.

✦ **Prep him for change.** Whenever possible, tell your child in advance about upcoming changes in his routine. This will give him a chance to think about and ease himself into the shift.

APPROACH TO LEARNING

The learning of many seven-year-olds is an interesting mix of moving forward and holding back. While they can be curious and eager to explore new ideas, have new experiences, and learn new skills, at the same time they may want to practice things over and over to get them perfect. And they may be afraid of making mistakes. Second-graders are very industrious; they love building and inventing things. When learning about new things, they want real-life, hands-on experiences; they want to see, touch, do, and talk. Books feed their lively imaginations, but are only beginning to be a meaningful source of new information. Because of their desire to be independent and in control of their actions and choices, seven-year-olds often like to work on learning activities by themselves or with just one other child. They may become frustrated when their first or second effort is not successful; patient adults can help them work through problems and feel like capable learners.

FROM SCHOOL TO HOME

Second grade offers your child increasingly challenging opportunities to meet her growing zest for learning. For one thing, she engages in multi-step projects, such as watching her classroom's pet guinea pig, asking questions about it, researching guinea pigs, and writing about what she has learned. For another, she tries new activities, such as writing poems and stories or choosing to work with children she doesn't usually play with. She will stay focused on a complicated writing, building, or art project, working on it over several days until it is finished. And she'll seek additional information about a topic of interest by going to the library, asking someone who is an expert, or searching the Web. She may also offer a friend several suggestions, rather than just one, for solving a problem.

Your seven-year-old will be excited about what she is learning in school and want to continue her study at home. She'll also work hard to perfect an at-home craft project. You'll hear her express clear ideas about activities she wants to try, such as playing a particular game or reading a certain book. She may read longer books over several days. She'll find new ways to play old games and make new routines for her family jobs. And don't be surprised if she works several weeks on a secret outdoor hideout.

It's Your Turn

You encourage your child's quest for knowledge when you:

+ **Create a learning environment for her.** Read, talk, make things, and go places together.

+ **Solicit solutions.** Ask your child to suggest ways to solve problems.

+ **Cheer her "stick-to-itiveness."** Praise your child for finishing projects that require patience and persistence.

+ **Teach your child a new skill:** fishing, sewing, basketball, card games. Remember to be patient. Your child wants perfection quickly and may become frustrated.

+ **Get excited about school.** Let your child know you think school and learning are important by asking her questions about her day at school, helping with homework, looking at the work she brings home, and going to school for conferences and special events.

+ **Instigate ingenuity.** Encourage your child to think of more than one way to do things and then to try them out.

+ **Model a lust for learning.** Be a curious learner yourself: Notice and talk about things; read books, newspapers, magazines; listen to and talk about the news.

+ **Facilitate her passions.** Help your child pursue an expressed interest. If she wonders how engines work, for example, get relevant books from the library, visit a local car repair shop, or watch an electrician repair a vacuum cleaner.

+ **Join her in a project.** Help your child make something she's interested in—an animal out of clay, a shoebox diorama of her room, a musical instrument, an original book with words and drawings about something she has done.

+ **Encourage pleasure reading.** Help your child find other books by an author she has enjoyed reading.

+ **Create together.** With your child, put on a puppet show, write a poem about an experience or feeling, make up your own dance, keep a journal together.

INTERACTIONS WITH OTHERS

Both in and out of school, second-graders are learning how to cooperate, play fairly, and work through conflict peacefully. They are beginning to understand how groups of people work together and how they need to act in groups. With a little encouragement, most seven-year-olds are able to share materials, take turns, and follow rules, as well as be kind and respectful to others. Their capacity to compromise in order to solve conflicts is growing, as is their overall independence. But they still need adults close by to praise them and guide them through difficult situations.

Friends are becoming very important to second-graders, who strive to be accepted by other children. In large groups there may be a lot of arguing about rules and who is boss, but in smaller groups children this age are usually cooperative and flexible, especially if an adult is nearby.

From School to Home

Social interaction is a key part of a second-grade classroom. Your child regularly works in groups of three or four—building things, performing in skits, creating art, reading books. He participates in group discussions, such as class meetings, and in class projects, such as cleaning up or putting on a play. He knows to follow the rules and be a good sport when playing indoor and outdoor games. As he interacts with other children, he learns to use words and phrases to express his feelings: "I don't like it when you call me names. Please stop." He is able to discuss suggestions for settling a playground conflict during a class meeting.

You'll find that your seven-year-old is increasingly capable of playing with siblings or friends around the house without getting into major disagreements. He may even talk through a problem with a sibling or pal instead of fighting about it. You may see him suggest a fair way to choose teams or help explain the rules to other children when playing games in the neighborhood. He can now enjoy and function well in out-of-school groups, such as scouts, sports teams, or religious groups. His growing sense of empathy allows him to be sympathetic and caring when another person is hurt or upset.

It's Your Turn

To foster your child's social skills and his enjoyment of interactive learning:

+ **Let him play freely—but be there.** Arrange unstructured play time with other children, and stick close by to help with any tough social issues that might arise.

+ **Brief him on the social basics.** Prepare your child for peer-group interaction by talking about how to act and what to do when problems come up.

+ **Be mindful of manners.** Remind your child to use the rules of politeness and respect that he's already learned when he talks to others.

+ **Praise his social skills.** Notice and compliment your child's efforts to be pleasant and positive with other children and adults.

+ **Go for more than the win.** Encourage your child to focus on aspects of sports and games other than winning and losing—learning new skills, cheering on the other players, working together on a goal.

+ **Teach your child to speak up for himself.** Suggest that he use "I" sentences when things make him angry: "I don't like it when you grab my markers. Please don't do it."

+ **Foster respect for differences.** Talk with your child about how people can have varying opinions and still be friends.

+ **Read and discuss books about social behavior**—stories that include characters playing, living, or working together in helpful, cooperative ways and settling conflicts peacefully. Second-graders love Patricia Reilly Giff's *Kids of the Polk Street School* series. Ask your local librarian for book recommendations.

+ **Model healthy conflict-resolution behavior.** Set an example for your child by using calm talk and compromise to settle issues.

+ **Let him settle his own disputes.** Give your child suggestions for working out conflicts; avoid always being the umpire and working them out for him.

+ **Find alternatives to violence.** Talk frankly about other ways to deal with conflicts besides physical force.

+ **Have television and film talks.** When characters have conflicts, discuss how they deal with them. Ask your child if he has other ideas for solving problems.

+ **Brainstorm.** Together, come up with several ways to resolve real or pretend conflicts so your child sees that different solutions for a single issue are possible.

CHAPTER 10

Language and Literacy

✦

All aspects of the language arts are emphasized in the second-grade classroom—reading, vocabulary, spelling, writing, listening, and conversation. These skills are not only vital in their own right, they are also essential for every other subject. Story time, quiet reading, word and spelling games, creative play with stories—these are just some of the ways second-graders learn language and literacy skills.

Developing positive attitudes towards literacy activities through stories, reading aloud, independent reading, listening centers, and word games is essential for second-graders' success at reading and writing, as well as their ability to listen for meaning in conversations and being able to put thoughts and ideas into words. Second-graders' growth in language and literacy can be seen in these areas:

Listening and speaking

Literature and reading

Writing and spelling

LISTENING AND SPEAKING

Seven-year-olds love to talk, especially with their friends! Their language ability is growing in detail and description. They listen with purpose to learn what other people think, gather information, be entertained, and know what to do in certain situations. They work to better understand what they hear and often ask questions when they want to know more.

Children this age are also learning to talk differently in different situations. For example, when they talk on the telephone to a grandparent, they use different words and tone of voice than when they talk in person to friends or parents. They are increasingly aware of how to use their voice and words for a specific purpose, such as giving information, persuading a listener, entertaining someone, or offering an opinion.

From School to Home

Your second-grader has plenty of opportunity to practice her growing language skills in school. For example, she listens to the teacher give a series of directions for homework, remembers the instructions, and carries them out at home. She listens to classmates tell stories or give reports and then asks questions or makes comments in response. Your child is more and more able to speak up during class discussions and offer an opinion or add more information. She can also explain to the class how she found the answer to a particular problem. She may take part in a class skit or puppet show and make up lines as the show progresses.

Of course, listening and speaking fill your child's home life. You'll find that she can listen to stories for lengthy periods of time and over a number of days or weeks; and she'll remember the plots and characters. She's able to clearly describe events that happened at school or in the neighborhood. She now participates more fully than ever in family discussions. Your savvy second-grader can tell riddles and jokes and use puns to entertain people. And she'll listen to music simply for her own pleasure and relaxation.

It's Your Turn

To further her listening and speaking skills:

+ **Read and chat.** Encourage your child to talk or ask questions about books you read to her.

+ **Show her how *you* listen.** Set an example by paying attention, asking questions, and making relevant comments.

+ **Lay out a plan.** Give your child clear three- and four-step directions for a task, and ask her if she understands before she starts to carry them out.

+ **Have her use her ears without her eyes.** Encourage your child to listen to music, the radio, or books on tape as an alternative to television.

+ **Do it in the car, too.** Listen to music or books on tape during a long ride.

+ **Play story games.** Create add-a-line stories: One of you starts a story, another adds a little to it, and so on until the story comes to an end.

+ **...and concentration games.** Try "Grandmother's Trunk," in which your child has to listen to what goes in the trunk, remember it all, repeat the items, and then add another.

+ **Listen to the world together.** Take listening walks around the neighborhood, and keep a list of everything you hear.

+ **Get into the rhythm.** Recite nursery rhymes or make up poems together to help train your child's ear for the rhythm of words.

+ **Have her make up picture-book stories.** Borrow wordless books from the library and make up stories to go with them. Good examples of storybooks with no words are *A Boy, a Dog and a Frog*, by Mercer Mayer, and *The Snowman*, by Raymond Briggs.

+ **Involve her in family chats.** Make sure your child gets a chance to speak during family conversations.

+ **Watch her act it out.** Be an audience for your child's original skits, puppet shows, and jokes. Encourage her to use descriptive details in her stories. All of this will serve to increase her improvisational word power.

+ **Help her to talk about herself.** Ask your child to explain her feelings, thoughts, and opinions. If she is hesitant, suggest words she can use to describe what's in her heart and mind—happy, sad, glad, mad, excited, angry, interesting, silly, smart, beautiful, good, bad.

+ **Promote her public voice.** Encourage your child to speak to store clerks and servers in restaurants and to answer and use the telephone.

LITERATURE AND READING

Most second-graders learn to read independently. They continue to use many of the skills they began to use in first grade, and they also learn new ones. They look at the pictures and listen to what the words mean; they sound out new words; they read ahead when they get stuck and come back to try again; they listen for which words make sense and sound right; they memorize many words.

Children love using their new skills to go through many different kinds of print. They read storybooks, books with facts in them, and the fine print in games, comics, food boxes, traffic signs, billboards, and ad posters. They show that they understand what they read when they tell about the action in a story, share some information, laugh at the funny parts, or use what they read in their drawing or writing. As good as they are at reading on their own, however, seven-year-old readers still love it when others read to them.

FROM SCHOOL TO HOME

In school your child reads many things for many reasons every day: He reads stories to classmates or younger students, reads along with books on tape, reads books and writes book reports, reads factual books and writes research reports, reads songs and poetry, and reads messages and signs. His teacher will ask him to read aloud, try out new reading skills, answer questions about what he's read, or summarize stories in his own words. In response to reading certain books, he may draw pictures about the material, act out characters, create a puppet show from the stories, or write follow-up stories. He borrows books from the school library for quiet reading time in class or at home.

Ask your child why he liked or didn't like a book, and he'll be able to express his opinion. His increasing skill enables him to read aloud at home, using the pictures, letters, and story clues to help him. When you read to him, he'll read along quietly or silently; he's apt to ask questions about what is being read and answer questions you ask. He'll have a collection of favorite books he reads again and again. And he can, of course, play board games that have words on cards or on the board.

It's Your Turn

Reading is crucial to your child's learning success. To nurture his lifelong love of reading:

+ **Enjoy books with your child every day.** Listen to your child read or read to him daily, even if just for a few minutes.

+ **...and discuss them.** Talk about books your child reads and show interest in the content.

+ **...and question him about them.** Ask your child about what he reads: "What part was your favorite? Why? Was there anything in that book that reminded you of your life? Was there a part that made you mad, happy, sad, or afraid? What did you like about the words? What did you like about the pictures?"

+ **Stock up!** Keep a good supply of children's books on hand, either borrowed from the library or bought. (Check out the Web to buy books at a discount.)

+ **Go over the newspaper.** Help your child read his favorite parts of the daily news.

+ **Let him read all kinds of things.** Encourage your child to read lots of different kinds of print: game directions, recipes, owners' manuals, and so on.

+ **Show him *you* love to read.** Read for your own pleasure, and let your child see it. Then talk about your books with him. As you model *your* appreciation of reading, you'll encourage *his.*

+ **Have him read up on his passions.** Support your child's special interests by finding books about his hobby, favorite sport, favorite animal, and so on.

+ **Focus on authorship.** Encourage your child to read several books written by the same person, and then talk about the writer and the writing.

+ **Get him into a series.** Help your child become interested in a group of books by reading the first of a well-written series to him. Check with your local librarian for worthy series suggestions.

WRITING AND SPELLING

By the time they're in second grade, children know that writing is a powerful way to share their ideas, feelings, and knowledge. Their writing begins to look and sound more conventional. They are learning to use capital and lower-case letters correctly; they usually write in full sentences; and they know that a period or some other punctuation goes at the end of a sentence. Second-graders are also becoming more aware of conventional spelling. They have memorized some common words but they continue to invent their own spelling for less familiar words. When they reread their writing they often recognize a misspelled word and ask for help in making it right.

Seven-year-olds still have a hard time organizing and focusing their writing, which tends to ramble and, at times, lack sense. Nonetheless, they are becoming more confident writers who respond well to learning rules and looking up words in a children's dictionary.

FROM SCHOOL TO HOME

Your child has many opportunities every day to read in her classroom and to write for a variety of purposes: journals, stories, poems, letters, skits, riddles, reports, signs, posters, newsletter articles. She organizes stories and reports to include beginnings and endings and to maintain focus. She may use "story maps" or outlines to help plan and organize her writing. Your second-grader now uses capital and lower-case letters as well as basic punctuation marks correctly. She can find out how to spell words by looking on a list in the classroom or in a beginner's dictionary, or asking a friend for help. And she may work with a classmate to look for and fix misspelled words in a piece of writing.

At home your child probably writes notes or cards to family members, makes additions to shopping lists, and prints signs for her bedroom door. To enhance her drawings, she may add two or three sentences to tell a simple story about what is happening. She may also write short notes in a diary or journal about things that happen each day. She'll attempt to spell certain words as she writes by saying them out loud and sounding out what she hears; she may then write "bisket" for basket, "pinsl" for pencil, or "bilding" for building.

It's Your Turn

Help build her writing and spelling skills:

- ✦ **Stock up on supplies.** Keep an ample selection of drawing and writing implements for your child to use.

- ✦ **Give her simple tasks**—short, easy writing jobs, such as, "Would you please put *butter* on the shopping list?"

- ✦ **Have her pen notes.** Encourage your child to write greeting cards, thank-you notes, and letters to relatives who live far away.

- ✦ **Hear her words.** Listen to your child read what she has written, and give her praise and gentle suggestions for improvement.

- ✦ **Discuss the way writers write.** As you read together, ask questions, such as, "Dr. Seuss likes to make up words, doesn't he? What are your favorites?"

- ✦ **Be authors together.** Make up and write stories to go with family photographs or pictures from magazines.

- ✦ **Focus on the basics.** Point out features of writing—interesting words, good descriptions, punctuation—as you read together; encourage your child to add these elements to her writing.

- ✦ **Play word games with your child:** word scrambles, crossword puzzles, "Junior Scrabble," "Boggle."

- ✦ **Make a word book.** Help your child keep a personal dictionary of words she is learning to spell.

- ✦ **Sound it out together.** Show her how to hear all of the parts, or syllables, of a word she is trying to spell: "How many parts does *umbrella* have? Sound out each part and write the sounds you hear."

- ✦ **Be gentle.** Avoid being too strict about spelling with your seven-year-old. You don't want your child to stop writing for fear of spelling a word wrong.

- ✦ **Spell the alphabet.** From *A* to *Z*, have your child try to spell a word starting with each letter.

- ✦ **Let her fly solo.** Encourage your child to try spelling words on her own rather than asking you how to spell them. And then appreciate what she has done without criticizing or correcting her.

CHAPTER 11

Mathematical Thinking

✦

Second-graders are learning more complex patterning formats (extending, creating, and so on) and mathematical language (ordinal, matrix, attributes), as well as place value, geometry, and much more. Excitement about their growing understanding of numbers and their relationships is essential to their continued growth in mathematical thinking. Helping seven-year-olds see how much mathematical concepts are a part of their every day lives helps them feel at home with more complicated mathematical concepts and strategies. Their progress can be seen in four areas:

Patterns and relationships

Numbers and their use

Geometry, spatial relations, and measurement

Probability and statistics

PATTERNS AND RELATIONSHIPS

Many complicated math ideas have to do with understanding patterns and relationships. Second-graders are becoming more experienced at seeing and making patterns. They draw patterns; they hear patterns in music. They see patterns in numbers when they count by 2s or fill in the series 3, 6, __, 12, __, 18. They also detect patterns in nature. And they are able to see multi-directional patterns—for example, in the squares of a crossword puzzle or while playing "Tic-Tac-Toe."

For seven-year-olds, understanding mathematical relationships involves being able to sort objects in different ways: by color, size, shape, texture, and so on. They can now describe the rules they use for sorting—"I sorted these buttons by the number of holes they have"— and compare the sizes of the groups they sort — "There are five more buttons with four holes than there are buttons with two holes." In addition, they are learning to arrange objects sequentially: tallest to shortest, heaviest to lightest; this is another important part of understanding relationships.

FROM SCHOOL TO HOME

Your child's classroom experience is influenced in a big way by patterns and relationships. He has many opportunities to create and make pictures of patterns with blocks, stickers, and drawings. He will move from simple patterns (ABAB or ABCABC) to more complex patterns (AABCCAABCC or ABBCCABBCC). And he's ready to find the missing numbers in a pattern: 15, 13, 11, __, 7, __, 3,__. Your second-grader sorts many kinds of objects in many different ways—by size, shape, color, weight, function—and records his work in pictures or words. He uses sorting in useful ways, such as grouping puzzle pieces before starting the puzzle. He may collect information over a period of time and compare his findings at the end of that period. He may record the temperature each day at 9:00 a.m. and then find the coldest and warmest days, the difference between the two, and so forth.

Patterns will also be prevalent throughout your seven-year-old's daily life. He'll notice patterns all around him: in the sand by the ocean, in a grocery store display, in the petals of flowers, in his favorite music. He may decorate his artwork with patterned borders or make up gymnastic routines that use repeated movement patterns. Collector that he is, he is surrounded by all kinds of items that beg to be sorted in many different ways—baseball cards, stuffed animals, rocks, or shells.

It's Your Turn

To promote your child's pattern and sorting perceptions:

+ **Try some fancy footwork.** Make up a pattern of steps and body movements as you dance together to favorite music.

+ **Listen for patterns.** Together, find repeating patterns in songs, poems, and chants.

+ **Engage in a pattern game.** Play "Guess the Pattern": One of you makes a pattern on paper, with blocks, or in a song, and the other tries to guess what it is.

+ **Offer him the creative-rule challenge:** Have your child sort objects; then try to guess the rules he used, challenging him to make it harder and harder for you to guess.

+ **Put him on pattern duty.** Give your child household sorting jobs: laundry, groceries, coins.

+ **Let him organize it.** Ask your child to arrange a collection of toys, a pile of books, or the contents of a tool drawer.

+ **Say "buzz."** Pick a number between 1 and 10—say, 7—and start counting, taking turns saying the numbers. Every time one of you comes to a number with a 7 in it (7, 17, 27) the person says "buzz" instead of the number.

+ **Go on road hunts.** Make up traveling games that involve looking for patterns or categories of objects (red things, round things, things that are bigger than the car) along the roadside.

+ **Discuss jigsaw strategies.** Assemble jigsaw puzzles together and talk about the different ways you go about fitting pieces together, such as matching colors, looking for certain shapes, and so on.

+ **Go beyond Xs and Os.** Play "Tic-Tac-Toe" using a variety of symbols. When you see the games shape up in different designs, your child will get a better sense of the patterns the games make.

NUMBERS AND THEIR USE

Second-graders continue to build on what they have learned about numbers in kindergarten and first grade. They count more and more objects, and they read and write higher numbers. They compare numbers (50 is more than 43); they learn how to double numbers and to use doubling strategies for adding (5 plus 5 equals 10, so 5 plus 6 must equal 11); they learn more about number families (8 plus 2 equals 10, so 10 minus 8 equals 2); they learn place value (76 is made up of seven 10s and six 1s).

The ability to explain how problems are solved becomes very important, because it helps your second-grader understand how she got an answer. As math problems become more difficult, your child needs to go through several steps to reach an answer. Explaining the process helps her learn the specific words needed to talk about math.

FROM SCHOOL TO HOME

Your seven-year-old continues to count, read, write, and compare numbers every day in school. She may play number games with dice or she may be the scorekeeper when playing games—adding up scores as the game goes along, then comparing scores at the end to find out how close the players were. She solves word problems: "You have a dollar and you spend 70 cents on a snack. How much money will you get back in change?" She uses place-value blocks to show how many 10s and how many 1s are in a given number. And how does she show how to share 48 pieces of candy with 24 classmates? She might draw a picture of it. She uses small blocks or other objects to figure out how many people would be in a group if the class was divided into three groups.

Numbers will keep your child busy at home, too. She may cut a piece of fruit or a sandwich into equal pieces (halves, quarters, or eighths) or keep score in a family card game. You'll find that she enjoys making number guesses: "I think there are 50 M&Ms in the package." And watch her count her money to figure out how much more she'll need to buy something she wants.

IT'S YOUR TURN

To keep your child counting:

+ **Look for the big ones.** Have your child read numbers on signs, on buildings, or in books.

+ **Let her keep score.** Play card or board games with your child and ask her to add up the points.

+ **Throw math questions at her.** Create word problems for your child to solve: "If everyone in our family has three hats, how many hats do we have in all?"

+ **Let her "guesstimate":** "Do you think this pumpkin weighs more or less than you weigh? By how much?"

+ **Play with money.** Count, add, and subtract dimes, nickels, and pennies with your child.

+ **...and play with play money.** Have your child make pretend money and then play "grocery store" together; offer her money to pay for various items and make sure she gives you the correct change.

+ **Let her be the banker.** Have your child give you the amounts of play money you ask for, figure out your new balance after you make deposits or withdrawals, and make change for you when you give her more than the intended amount.

+ **Do a "digit-al" car trip.** Look for the numbers 1 to 100 in signs and license plates, or tally how many cows, dogs, cats, trucks, vans, or trailers you see.

+ **Play a numbers game:** With each letter of the alphabet having a numerical value—A = 1, B = 2, C = 3, etc.—spell words and add up the value of the letters to get a word score. See who can get the most points out of five words.

+ **Encourage her shopping smarts.** Give your child problems to solve while grocery shopping: "If this watermelon weighs 5 pounds and you weigh 50 pounds, how much more do you weigh?"

+ **Give her the answer.** Tell your child a number (15, for example) and ask her to think of problems that have that number as the answer (10 + 5; 3 + 12; 17 - 2; 20 - 5).

+ **Check her answers.** Ask your child how she figured out the math problem she just solved.

GEOMETRY, SPATIAL RELATIONS, AND MEASUREMENT

Second graders increase their understanding of mathematical forms and relationships as they build and design with a variety of materials. They learn to talk about shapes and how they are made. They learn to organize shapes and put them together to create designs and solve problems. They are beginning to make complex structures that are balanced and symmetrical as well as three-dimensional. The more experience they have, the more they explain their thinking and actions.

Second-graders are also learning about increasingly complicated measurements, which include volume and speed as well as length and weight. They still use non-standard units of measure—hands, feet, blocks, strips of paper. But they are becoming more familiar with standard units of measure—inch, foot, yard, cup, pint, gallon. They are also ready to learn the basic units of time on the clock: hour and half hour. They now attempt to predict how much time it will take to do something and estimate quantities or the weight of objects.

FROM SCHOOL TO HOME

Your second-grader's school is a world rich with shapes, designs, and measurements. He interacts with this world as he looks for shapes in the school building. He creates a building using these shapes. He might play a game like "Guess the Shape," in which he'll ask, "What has three straight lines that come together at three corners?" He could use rubber bands on a geoboard to practice geometric ideas of reflection, symmetry, and balance. Your child estimates weights of small objects, then uses a scale to check his estimates. He might also build a ramp with blocks and then use a stop watch or a wrist watch with a second hand to measure the time it takes for a car to roll down various angles of slope.

At home your child points out shapes he sees around him: "The roof has two triangles on each end and two rectangles on the sides." He also finds shapes around the house to trace and use to make designs. He might construct paper airplanes or simple origami forms by folding paper and then explain how he did it: "You start with a square and fold it in half so you have two triangles." His Lego or block structures will include new and varied shapes, angles, and symmetry. He can now use a clock or watch to tell that it is almost time for dinner or bed.

IT'S YOUR TURN

Watch things shape up for your child as you:

+ **Make and talk shapes.** Work with your child to make designs out of small shape blocks; encourage him to use shape words to describe each design and how he made it.

+ **Have a quilting bee.** Help your child make a small quilt by cutting and stitching fabric squares and triangles.

+ **Give him a grid.** Supply your child with graph paper to color the squares into designs.

+ **Practice origami.** Get a book on origami from the library to learn together how to fashion these wonderful shapes from paper.

+ **Shape with scrap wood.** Get wood pieces of varied sizes and shapes at a lumber yard (they often give them away); glue them together to create bridges, buildings, or designs; leave them natural or paint them.

+ **Slice bread.** Have your child determine how many different shapes a sandwich can be cut into (three rectangles, six squares, two triangles, etc.).

+ **Play with homemade Tinkertoys.** Together, construct two- and three-dimensional shapes out of toothpicks connected with little balls of clay, whole dried peas soaked in water overnight, or miniature marshmallows.

+ **Teach him to measure.** Help your child use and read measuring tools: scale, tape measure, measuring cups, kitchen timer.

+ **Then let him measure up.** Ask your child to help you measure things around the house: laundry soap, cooking ingredients, the temperature on the thermostat, his weight on the bathroom scale, the height of a lamp.

+ **Talk measurements.** Ask your child questions that will encourage him to use measuring words when he answers: "How big was this place you're telling me about?"

+ **Make time to tell time.** Make sure there is a clock with hands in the house so your child can learn to read hours and minutes.

+ **Play games with a time limit:** "How many words can you write in 5 minutes?"; "You have 30 seconds to take your turn at checkers."

+ **Mark miles.** Teach your child how to read the odometer in the car; have him figure out distances by comparing the beginning mileage with the ending mileage.

+ **Have him keep a schedule.** Let your child have his own calendar to keep track of the days, weeks, months.

PROBABILITY AND STATISTICS

Probability and statistics may sound complicated, but for second-graders it means collecting and keeping track of information. Children enjoy taking surveys (finding out what ice-cream flavors people like) and keeping tallies to collect information (making a mark under the right bird name each time one of those birds is seen at the bird feeder). They are learning how to make different kinds of graphs (picture graphs, bar graphs, line graphs) to show information to other people. They are also learning to read graphs and then draw conclusions and make predictions from them.

FROM SCHOOL TO HOME

In school your seven-year old uses statistical information to make predictions: She may, for instance, roll a die 20 times, tally how many times a 6 is rolled, compare her results to those of other people, and then predict how many 6s might come up in 40 rolls. She uses data to shape her choices: She may make a graph that shows how high different kinds of kites flew and then, based on information from the graph, choose a certain kind of kite to build. She takes surveys and graphs the results: For example, she could survey her classmates about numbers of brothers and sisters and show the results in a picture graph. Or she'll measure the growth of a seedling and track its growth on a line graph. Your child makes guesses or estimates: She and her classmates will guess how many dry beans are in a jar, graph the guesses, and then count the beans to find out who made the best estimates.

When your family attends a sports event, your child may keep track of scores and how many points different players make. She might also keep track of how much the family pet eats and then chart how much it weighs. She may even conduct a poll to see what game your family wants to play, or she'll record on a bar graph the number of times each family member has to be called before they get out of bed on school mornings. You may also see her study the weather and temperature chart in the newspaper.

It's Your Turn

To nurture your young statistician:

- **Have her keep track.** Help your child collect information and organize it on a graph: the daily temperature, the colors of cars that drive by, the number and kinds of stuffed animals she has, the types of shells she collects.

- **Talk about the data.** Encourage your child to use words to describe graphs and charts she makes: less than, more than, equal, the most, the least, shortest, longer, longest.

- **Make sense of the media.** Show her how to read charts and graphs in newspapers and magazines.

- **Chart a family plan.** Ask your child to make charts of the family's weekly schedules or assigned household chores.

- **Help her manage her money.** Have your child keep a record of how she spends her allowance or how much money she earns doing small jobs.

- **Watch plants grow.** After planting a garden or potting a bulb, help your child graph the ongoing growth progress.

- **Track the weather.** Together, set up a weather graph and chart the number of days in a month that it rained, snowed, was cloudy, or was sunny; then transfer the monthly results onto a yearly graph.

- **Make a meal plan.** Chart family menus for a week to identify how many foods were served in each food group (vegetables, fruit, protein, dairy, and so on).

- **Record reading data.** Help your child set up a chart to tally the books she reads each month. Organize this into categories, such as Fiction, Biography, and Science.

- **Keep on guessing.** Estimate the number of cookies in a package, the number of chocolates in a box, the number of squares in your walkway to the street. Count the various items to see who came closest to guessing correctly.

CHAPTER 12

Scientific Thinking

✦

Discovery abounds in the second-grade classroom. The teacher's instruction, supplemented with a wide variety of science projects, helps children acquire new information as well as new ways of thinking about the world. They are also learning more ways to test and make discoveries on their own. Critical thinking, problem-solving, and curiosity are at the heart of early learning in scientific thinking. Second-graders' growth in scientific thinking can be seen in two ways:

**Observing, investigating,
and questioning**

**Predicting, explaining, and
forming conclusions**

OBSERVING, INVESTIGATING, AND QUESTIONING

Second-graders are good observers. They use their eyes, ears, nose, and fingers to take in information and find answers to their questions about the world. By age seven, children observe details that they might have overlooked in the past. They realize that careful, systematic observation can help them find answers. The questions second-graders ask are becoming more specific. Instead of simply asking, "Why?" children are beginning to ask, "What would happen if...?" or, "How can I find out...?" Second-graders are ready to use new tools, such as scales, thermometers, magnifying lenses, and binoculars, to help them make their observations.

FROM SCHOOL TO HOME

The second-grade classroom is filled with opportunities for observation and discovery. Your child regularly records observations of plants, animals, insects, or the trees outside. He may collect, describe, and categorize data that was gathered on a rock hunt; then he may carefully draw and describe one of the rocks and decide which group it belongs to. Your seven-year-old uses scientific tools, such as binoculars for discovering whether the birds at the feeder eat the shells of the sunflower seeds. He asks questions about scientific information in books: "How can air pollution be measured if it is invisible?" He also may design experiments to answer questions, such as, "How do hamsters learn their way through mazes?"

You'll see your child show curiosity about animals, outer space, how machines work, or other science topics. He may find a cricket outside and keep it in a jar for a while to try to find out what it looks like when it chirps. He'll ask questions about why things change or how things are made and want to find answers in books or by conducting experiments. He'll check the thermometer or listen to weather forecasts before deciding what to wear to school on a particular day. Overall, real-life subjects will spur real-life questions: "How do they build bridges?"; "What happens if we put two eggs instead of one in the pancake batter?"

"It's great to see how science activities help your child see things in his own unique way."

IT'S YOUR TURN

To bring out the scientist in your second-grader:

+ **Be on the lookout.** Take walks with your child and encourage careful watching and listening as you go.

+ **Play describing games:** "Pretend you've seen a car, and try to tell me what it looks like so I can recognize it."

+ **Give him the tools.** Encourage your child to use binoculars, a scale, a thermometer, a magnifying glass, and other science tools.

+ **Encourage experiments.** Help your child set up simple experiments so he can answer some of his own questions: "What does a spider's leg look like?"; "How does a leaf get food?"; "Does water take up more space when it is liquid or frozen?"

+ **Have him see things in a new light.** Take a careful look at familiar objects—a tree, your car, the room—and both of you try to notice something about it that you've never noticed before; suggest that your child describe the object or space as specifically as possible.

+ **Notice the little things.** Together, look in the mirror and draw self-portraits; encourage your child to notice small details, such as how his eyes and nose line up with his ears, how much forehead shows beneath his hair, the shape of his lips, the lines or dimples on his skin.

+ **Inspire his questions with yours.** Set an example by asking probing questions: "What would happen if...?"; "How could we find out about...?"

+ **Let him find the way.** Whenever possible, encourage your child to discover answers to his questions instead of telling him what the answers might be.

+ **Have science challenges.** One of you ask a question and write it down on a piece of paper; list everything each of you knows related to the question (guesses as well as facts). After an agreed-upon number of days, share what each of you has written down about the question. You'll be amazed at how much two people know!

+ **Scrutinize and sketch.** Encourage your child to draw what he sees when he looks at his thumbprint through a magnifying glass or draw the differences between a maple leaf and an oak leaf.

+ **Play "Twenty Questions."** Think of an object, animal, or person and give your child 20 questions to figure out your selection.

PREDICTING, EXPLAINING, AND FORMING CONCLUSIONS

Answering such questions as "Why do you think this happened?" and "What did you learn from studying this?" is an important part of the scientific process. Younger children might give very imaginative answers, but second-graders are able to use their observations and the information they have learned from similar experiences to make rather educated and realistic predictions. For example, upon seeing a large bird, a second-grader might say, "That bird is big and I can see its beak. I think it's some kind of hawk." They are also becoming adept at explaining what has happened ("The cake puffed up because it was hot in the oven.") as well as what they think might happen in a similar situation ("Bread is like cake. It'll rise in the hot oven.").

FROM SCHOOL TO HOME

Your second-grader uses investigations to make predictions. For example, she observes a plant in class and then predicts what would happen if no one watered it. She now knows to use the word *predict* when answering questions about what she thinks will happen next. She can form conclusions about why cake batter rises in the oven after studying about yeast, dough, and other cooking processes. She also conducts experiments and explains her conclusions: She'll run wheel-toys down a ramp, observe which one went fastest, and explain why. And your child now describes her observations using shape, color, size, and texture words.

Around the house, all kinds of scientific processes will intrigue your seven-year-old. She may predict how long it will take ice cubes to freeze or explain why the robins are the first birds to fly north in the spring. She'll watch a bee collect pollen from a flower and explain that the bee collects as much it can hold in its stomach before flying back to its hive. She'll use prior experience to make some predictions: "If you put the egg into boiling water, it will break; I've seen it happen before." She now has the vocabulary to tell you about an experiment she did in school and describe what she learned. And she can explain to a younger sibling or other child how water gets into the faucets.

IT'S YOUR TURN

To encourage her good guesses:

✦ **Honor her theories.** Show appreciation for your child's predictions, even when they are unrealistic. Predictions are rarely accurate, and it takes courage to make them.

✦ **Query her predictions:** "How did you know which car would reach the bottom of the ramp first? What did you base your prediction on?"

✦ **...and her observations:** "Why do you think this happened?"; "What do you know now that you didn't know before?"

✦ **Help her learn the words.** Teach your child language that will help her explain her ideas more clearly. For example: The "slope" of a ramp is how steep it is; "evaporate" means changing form and being "absorbed" into the air.

✦ **Let her look it up.** Encourage your child to use books so she can compare her explanations with those of the experts.

✦ **Ask "Why?":** "Why do you think most people sleep at night?"; "Why don't birds fall off branches?"; "Why is it colder in the winter?" These questions will encourage your child to think and then explain her thinking.

✦ **Listen!** Show interest and curiosity in your child's scientific explanations and conclusions.

✦ **Be partners in science.** Do some experiments with your child to check out her predictions and yours: "Let's guess how long it will take this ice cube to melt and let it melt to see if we were right. Then we'll try it again and see if we can make more accurate predictions the second time."

✦ **Be "estimable."** Make a game of estimating, for example, how long it will take you to drive from home to the store. Keep a record of your predictions and check them to see how many times each of you were able to guess correctly.

✦ **Try a team science project.** For example, study star formations or plant growth with your child. Read together, make guesses about what happens next, check out observations and predictions.

✦ **Try it at home.** Find out what she is studying in science at school and do home research, experimentation, and documentation with her.

✦ **Prepare a scientific journal.** Together, keep a home diary of the scientific discoveries you and she make, perhaps entering one new discovery each week.

CHAPTER 13

Social Studies

✦

For seven-year-olds, social studies learning continues to focus on themselves, their families, and their communities. In addition, their studies expand to learning about other cultures and traditions. In this way they learn how customs and rules vary from one group to another, how the environment affects how we live, and how the past influences our lives today. Second graders' understanding of our world centers on two areas:

People and how they live their lives

How the past, the land, and people affect one another

PEOPLE AND HOW THEY LIVE THEIR LIVES

Second-graders are beginning to understand that the people in their families, class-room, and community are the same in some ways and different in other ways. They are able to see that people depend on each other and work at many different jobs, each important in its own way. They are beginning to study the different kinds of knowledge, skills, and tools people need to do their jobs. Seven-year-olds are also aware that people use simple as well as high-tech tools and machines at their work as well as in their homes.

Children this age are learning more about problems that come up when people are in groups. They study the need for rules and for leaders to help make group decisions. When second-graders help make classroom and family rules, they realize that good rules help protect people from being hurt or treated badly. They are beginning to learn how decisions are made in a democracy through discussion and voting.

FROM SCHOOL TO HOME

In class your child studies and compares the ways people help each other in fami-lies, schools, and communities. He asks questions about what people do in different kinds of jobs. He may interview different community workers and then write about what he has learned about their lives and jobs. He begins to see how tech-nology affects his life by visiting a business or office building and learning about dif-ferent machines used there. Your child and his second-grade classmates decide on classroom rules at the beginning of the year and discuss them as time goes along. They will vote on a classroom issue, such as where to go on a class trip. Your child may get to interview the school principal or a town leader about what it's like to be in charge.

Then your seven-year-old will come home and write a thank-you note to someone who is helpful in his school or community. He'll be curious about how much things cost and about how to earn money. And he'll want to learn about who invented the television, telephone, and computer, and explore how all this technol-ogy works. Don't be surprised if your child takes a leadership role with friends or siblings, organizing activities, settling arguments, or suggesting what to play.

It's Your Turn

To help her appreciate the people in her world:

✦ **Broaden her book horizons.** Read books about people who are different from you and discuss them with your child.

✦ **Voice respect for variety.** Help your child appreciate human differences—and how they are a part of human strength—so she is not afraid of people who are different from her.

✦ **Tap into international tunes.** Listen to music from many parts of the world and discuss its characteristics and variety with your child.

✦ **Make a people collage together.** Cut out pictures of different kinds of people from magazines; talk about the people as you turn the cut-outs into a collage of diversity.

✦ **Examine your images.** Look in a mirror with your child and list all the ways you and she are the same and different.

✦ **Say *buenos dias*, *bonjour*, or *ni hao*!** Learn how to say a few words in other languages. (These words are Spanish, French, and Mandarin Chinese for *hello*.)

✦ **Take her to work.** Show your child what you do and what tools, machines, and equipment you use.

✦ **Read about community spirit.** As you read books together, look for examples of how people in families, communities, and jobs work together to get things done.

✦ **Engage in occupational play.** Give your child props—a hard hat, a food-server's apron, a stethoscope, blueprint paper—and help her pretend to be different kinds of workers.

✦ **Make a "My Community Book":** In it, draw pictures of some of the people who help your community run smoothly.

✦ **Have her express thanks.** Help your child write a thank-you note to a community person or worker who has been helpful, such as a teacher, scout leader, coach, dentist, or store clerk.

✦ **Discuss rules**—why we need rules and laws and what life would be like without them. For example, ask what it would be like if we didn't have traffic laws.

✦ **Sketch out the rules.** Make a poster of family rules and let your child draw pictures to illustrate each one.

✦ **Play rule games**—such as "Simon Says" or "Follow the Leader"—so your child can know how it feels to sometimes be the leader and sometimes the follower.

HOW THE PAST, THE LAND, AND PEOPLE AFFECT ONE ANOTHER

Long before children can understand the importance of major historical events, they can understand how people lived in the past and how the past is connected to the present. Second-graders can appreciate the fact that they wouldn't be able to ride their bike if someone had not invented it, nor would they live where they do if their grandparents hadn't come to the United States fifty years ago.

A growing sense of geography helps seven-year-olds become increasingly competent at making maps and reading them. This fuels their realization that where people live (near water, on a mountain, in the city) affects the way they live. They see that geography, climate, type of land, or bodies of water influence people's jobs, clothing, and housing choices. They also begin to understand that when people build highways, cut down trees, or drive cars, there are both good and bad results.

FROM SCHOOL TO HOME

Your child develops historical perspective as she takes part in classroom "I remember when..." talks, in which children share memories of their own past. She might write and illustrate an autobiography while in the second grade. To understand changes in the land over time, she may interview a local historian about what used to be where the school is now or what the river was like before the dam was built. One class project may be to compare land, water, and lifestyles in different locations by exchanging letters and photographs with a pen pal in another part of the country. She may also make maps of the school, neighborhood, or park, using symbols to represent landmarks.

At home your child will talk and ask questions about her earlier years: "How old was I when...?" She'll also ask questions about how life was different when you were a child. Your young geographer will ask you to point out on the map where you are going for a family vacation. In addition, her growing environmental awareness may spur discussion about how hard it is to keep the school yard clean when children throw their lunch papers on the ground instead of in the trash cans. And she'll remind family members to recycle bottles, cans, and plastic containers.

It's Your Turn

You'll nurture her appreciation of the past and present when you:

+ **Look back.** Go through family albums and talk about people and places where you used to live or visit.

+ **Let her shape her life.** Help your child make a scrapbook or photo album of her own life.

+ **Check out historical fiction.** Read children's historical books—such as the Dear America or My Name Is America series books (Scholastic) or the Little House books—and talk about the differences between then and now.

+ **Have her question her elders.** Encourage your child to ask grandparents or other older people about the way life used to be.

+ **Seek out the past.** Visit historical museums or parks to see, touch, and learn about life in the past.

+ **Go back.** Talk about what life was like when there were no cars, electricity, or television, and maybe even try living without one or two of these commodities for a day.

+ **Get a bird's-eye view.** Take a walk up a hill or to a mountain top to talk about the geography of your area—rivers, mountains, lakes, forests, farming land, the city, the roads—and how they look from far away.

+ **Find it on the map.** Borrow an atlas from the library and show your child maps of the towns and cities near you or the roads you take when visiting a relative.

+ **Let her map out the route.** Help your child make a map to your house to send to a friend who is coming to visit.

+ **Make a map to the treasure.** Plan a treasure hunt for a special occasion, and let your child help you draw the maps showing where the treasures can be found.

+ **Let her get seasonal.** Ask your child to help you prepare for changing weather or seasons: Get out hurricane lamps; put on storm windows or snow tires; maintain fans and air conditioners.

+ **Encourage the environmentalist in her.** Talk about the need to recycle, to put trash in bins, to leave a picnic area the way you found it.

+ **Then let her be one.** Involve your child in community efforts to improve the environment: recycling, gardening, Earth Day projects.

CHAPTER 14

The Arts

✦

Art is not just drawing and painting. All arts and media (drawing, painting, sculpting, drama, dance, and music) are important for seven-year-olds to experience.When children create with clay or blocks, or even recycled materials, they are engaged in artistic activities, just as they are when they invent a skit, compose a song, or put together a dance routine. Second-graders are particularly adept at combining various art media with inventiveness and flexibility. They learn about the arts through:

Artistic expression

Artistic appreciation

ARTISTIC EXPRESSION

By the time children are in the second grade, their artwork has grown in realism and detail. Looking at their art helps adults understand what children are thinking. Second-graders are able to express their ideas in a variety of creative ways— through drawing, painting, sculpture, building, music, dance, drama, and poetry.

FROM SCHOOL TO HOME

As they gain new knowledge in school, second-graders use the arts as a way to make new information meaningful and real. Your seven-year-old will use his creativity with art materials to complement other school subjects. In science, he may discover a new way to use a paintbrush to get the special texture of leaves as part of a tree study, use colored pencils to design a scientific drawing of a shell or crystal, or combine an assortment of recycled materials to invent a "machine." In social studies, he may study and re-create past and present communities and use Legos, chairs, blankets, boards, blocks, boxes, and tires to build forts, castles, factories, and houses. He may make clay pots as part of a study of Native American life. Your child now combines multiple art forms with other forms of communication to express himself. For example, he might write a script, make puppets, and use sound effects to bring an imaginative story to life. He'll draw pictures about the people, places, and creatures he reads about in books. The artwork he does as part of school projects will encourage him to add creative details to drawings, such as boards on a house, lightning in the sky, jewelry on people, stripes and plaids on clothing, texture lines on tree bark, and borders around edges.

The increasing artistic ability and techniques he has discovered at school will spur him on at home. His creative instincts will lead him to add props and scenery to the skits and puppet shows he puts on, invent a set of dance steps to go with his favorite music, or make decorations on thank-you letters, greeting cards, or invitations.

IT'S YOUR TURN

To keep your seven-year-old's imagination and creative instincts thriving:

+ **Keep art supplies on hand**—different sizes of paper, scissors, bits of yarn and fabric, a stapler, a hole-puncher, Scotch tape, markers, crayons, pens, pencils, straws, Popsicle sticks, foil, wallpaper—and natural objects, such as leaves, pebbles, acorns—to make sure your child always has tools for creative expression.

+ **Show him *your* inner Rembrandt.** Find space and time to create works of art with your child.

+ **Show off his work.** To let him know that you appreciate his creative endeavors, put some of your child's artwork in frames or on cardboard backing and display it in a prominent place.

+ **Be his audience**—and enjoy his musical or dramatic productions.

+ **Compliment his creative thinking.** Praise your child's creative use of materials and solutions to problems: "What a clever way to use a paintbrush!"

+ **Write lyrics together.** Make up new words to familiar tunes.

+ **Indulge in creative freedom.** With your child, draw or paint by holding the crayon or paint brush with your toes, have fun with scribble art, make pinhole pictures, try fabric painting, create all sorts of partner pictures.

+ **Let one art form influence another.** Draw or paint with your child while listening to your favorite music.

+ **Craft cards.** Make holiday cards with your child to send to friends and relatives; let your child design them in his own creative way.

+ **Decorate the house.** Encourage your child to help make seasonal decorations for your home.

+ **Dance up a storm**—With your child, play music and cut loose!

+ **Re-create the past.** Make up a song, play, or story about a family vacation or celebration, a move to a new house, and so on.

ARTISTIC APPRECIATION

Not all second-graders are eager to be creative, but they can learn to watch and appreciate the creative expressions of others. Seven-year-olds are able to understand that the colors, shapes, sounds, and movements artists make are ways of expressing ideas, thoughts, and feelings. They can think about what the artist, dancer, or composer is trying to say.

FROM SCHOOL TO HOME

At school your child will have many opportunities to be an active art enthusiast. She can watch classmates create art and then appreciate their drawings, plays, sculptures, poems, and stories. She might develop an interest in the drawings of one particular book illustrator. Your second-grader can now talk about what various forms of art mean to her: She may listen to taped or live music and write about what it makes her think about; she may watch a play or dance performance and talk of what she did or did not like.

At home you'll hear your seven-year-old sing songs she learned at school, in scouts, or at religious school or services and ask what you think. She'll enjoy a dance production on television or music on the stereo. Interest in music may prompt your child to ask how to play a particular musical instrument, such as the piano or drums. As she looks at artwork in books she may ask questions or make comments, such as, "I wonder how the artist made that dragon." She is apt to become more appreciative of the artwork created by her siblings or friends.

It's Your Turn

To foster your child's love of the arts:

+ **Visit art galleries.** Take your child to museums or art galleries for short periods of time; ask her questions about what she sees; encourage her to ask questions of the staff.

+ **Muse about films.** See movies with your child and then discuss them: "What impressed you the most? What didn't you like? How did the background music help the story?"

+ **See live shows.** Go to arts performances geared toward children—plays, concerts, puppet shows, mime, dance concerts.

+ **Note those notes.** Stop and listen to the musician playing at the mall or on the street corner.

+ **Admire the architecture.** Pay attention to how buildings are designed and built, and discuss why an architect is an artist.

+ **...and the landscaping.** Notice the plantings around homes in your neighborhood. Try to figure out why you like some better than others.

+ **Read up on artists.** Borrow children's library books about artists, musicians, and dancers.

+ **Focus on book art.** Begin to notice the names of illustrators of the books you read together. Have her pick out her favorites and look for more of their work at the library or bookstore.

+ **Appreciate craftspeople.** Go to an arts-and-crafts fair to see different kinds of artists at work: potters, weavers, wood carvers.

+ **Discuss music-makers.** Watch a concert on television, and talk with your child about the music, the musicians, and the conductor.

+ **Don't let the parade pass her by.** Watch a local parade and point out to your child the skills of the clowns, majorettes, and musicians.

+ **Marvel at circus arts.** Attend a circus and help your child appreciate the talents of the various performers.

+ **See art in life.** Make a game of looking for evidence that an artist has been at work: on billboards, walls, newspapers, magazines, buildings, stamps, food packaging, and so on. Once you really start to look, you'll both be amazed!

CHAPTER 15

Physical Development and Health

✦

Physical development and health are very important to second-graders' growth, learning, and self-image. They need dexterity, coordination, and control for everything from sports and play to writing and artistic expression. Good health and physical skills give children confidence and allow them to learn at their best. It is also important that they be increasingly able to do things for themselves. Second-graders' physical development and personal health are seen in three areas:

Large-muscle development

Small-muscle development

Personal health and safety

LARGE-MUSCLE DEVELOPMENT

Second-graders are growing more and more confident and capable in their physical movements. They move more quickly than ever, and they're less likely to trip, fall, or lose their balance. They're also getting better at coordinating several body movements at once, such as jumping rope while turning in circles.

FROM SCHOOL TO HOME

School provides children with plenty of space and motivation for movement. Your seven-year-old carries things around the classroom without dropping them or bumping into people. He may do a simple dance step and play a rhythm instrument at the same time, or use his body to act out a story. Outdoors he plays catch or throws a ball or bean bag at a target. He climbs on the jungle gym. And he joins his classmates running on the playground—changing directions, stopping and starting suddenly, and swerving.

Ask your child to carry plates of food or full drinking glasses, and he will do so without dropping or spilling. Your active seven-year-old will use many different movements when playing outside: running, skipping, hopping, climbing, and jumping. Watch as he attempts physical challenges, such as jumping from heights or balancing on narrow surfaces. He now plays ball games that require coordination and concentration: tether ball, kickball, Whiffle ball. He might even try to ride his bike without holding the handlebars!

IT'S YOUR TURN

To keep your child on the move:

+ **Send him out and about.** Make sure your child gets plenty of active play—in the yard, at the park, in a gym. New research shows that in school, children get only a few minutes per day of high intensity activity, so lots of extra movement is important to your child's well-being.

+ **Get fit together.** Exercise with your child by jogging for short distances or going for walks.

+ **Stretch it out.** Do a few minutes of stretching exercises together in the morning.

+ **And try a fitness video.** Set up a 15-minute exercise video to work out to together a few times a week.

+ **Encourage extracurricular action.** Help your child get involved with organized sports or recreational activities.

+ **Hold a Family Olympics.** Include running races, hopping and jumping contests, obstacle courses, and so on.

+ **Track his speed.** Time your child to see how fast he can run a certain distance; keep a chart over time to see if he gets even faster.

+ **Don't forget the playground.** Your child isn't too old to swing on the swings, climb on the jungle gym, slide down the slide, and run around.

+ **Get to work!** Do outside chores with your child, such as raking leaves, shoveling snow, clearing brush, stacking wood, and gardening.

+ **Toss a few.** Play ball or throw a Frisbee together.

+ **Go the distance.** Do long jumps with your child to see who can jump farthest.

+ **Dance in your living room.** Turn on the music and each of you create new movements for the other to try to imitate.

SMALL-MUSCLE DEVELOPMENT

By second grade, children have gained strength in the small muscles of their hands, fingers, and wrists, and they can control the movements of these muscles. They are better than ever at coordinating their eyes and hands, which allows them to do more precise work: writing smaller letters, drawing details in pictures, sewing, and typing.

FROM SCHOOL TO HOME

Second-graders' hands are busy hands. In school your child uses staplers, hole-punchers, scissors, string, and tape to create two- and three-dimensional objects. She may use woodworking tools to build a box, a birdhouse, or a toy. She can type stories on a computer keyboard and write both capital and lower-case letters accurately. And she may use small shape blocks to make intricate designs, and then re-create them with paper cut-outs of the same shapes. Her work may be quite neat and precise.

At home your child will spend more time doing craft work with her hands: cutting, drawing, pasting, weaving. She may ask for help to sew a quilt for a doll's bed. She'll begin to put together pre-cut models independently. She'll also write more frequently and more legibly. Your seven-year-old can now tie her shoes tightly and use a spoon, fork, and knife with increasing ease.

"This book helps me realize that you have to allow your children to try. You have to give them the chance to make mistakes. Then you can step in and say, 'That's okay. Let me show you something that may make it easier the next time.'"

It's Your Turn

Her fingers will become more and more nimble if you:

+ **Keep supplies on hand.** Have scissors, staplers, hole-punchers, pencils, crayons, markers, colored paper, and scraps of cloth for your child to use. These supplies encourage not only creative arts expression, but greatly increase small-muscle development and skill.

+ **Applaud her skill.** Praise your child's efforts to do detailed work, even when it isn't perfect.

+ **Work your hands, too.** Draw and write with your child to let her know these are lifelong skills.

+ **Give her some chores**—those that work her small muscles, such as setting the table, pouring milk, peeling vegetables, writing things on the shopping list, tying her little sister's shoes, folding laundry.

+ **Get crafty together.** Make paper dolls, snowflakes, masks, and decorations with scissors, paper, and glue.

+ **Have her keep a journal.** Encourage your child to draw and write every day in a journal or diary.

+ **Play with your fingers**—games that require small motor skill, such as "Pick-Up-Sticks," marbles, cards, checkers.

+ **Follow the fold.** Make folded paper objects together, such as hats, boats, origami figures, and paper boxes.

+ **Let her participate in grown-up activities.** Include your child in any craft activities you enjoy doing, such as weaving, macrame, knitting, painting, decorating, and building models.

+ **Do it "sew" well.** Create simple sewing projects that you and your child can do together, such as making a simple costume or a pillow cover.

+ **Build things.** Share simple woodworking projects, such as building a bird feeder, book ends, or an extra closet shelf.

PERSONAL HEALTH AND SAFETY

Second-graders understand that the body needs certain things to work well: regular toilet use, washing, healthy food, rest, and so on. They also know the difference between safe and unsafe behaviors while playing outside, walking near streets, and doing day-to-day activities at home.

FROM SCHOOL TO HOME

Many school activities help your child learn about health and safety issues. He studies the human body and takes part in a stretching and exercise program. He may write a report that involves interviewing a variety of health professionals. In class your second-grader thinks about and discusses nutrition and the foods from various groups that he eats every day. The class may practice simple first aid, such as cleaning and covering wounds or putting ice on bruises. He'll also take part in safety exercises, such as fire drills and bus evacuations.

Your child understands rules of hygiene, so he washes his hands after using the toilet, before meals, or when helping with food preparation. He has learned to brush his teeth in the morning and at night. He also has learned that dressing appropriately affects his health and comfort, so he listens to the weather forecast to decide what to wear to school. Your maturing seven-year-old takes safety to heart as he looks both ways before crossing the street, wears a helmet when riding a bike, and wears a seat belt when in the car. And while he rides with you in the car he'll comment on safe-driving rules.

"This book encourages parents to sit down with their children and gives them ideas about things to do. When you have all the ingredients, you can do it!"

It's Your Turn

To help him take care of himself:

- ✦ **Stay healthy and safe yourself.** Model good habits and practices as an example for your seven-year-old.

- ✦ **Give him the thumbs-up.** Praise your child's hygiene efforts (washing his hands, brushing his teeth, blowing his nose and throwing the soiled tissue into the wastebasket).

- ✦ **Offer a bit more encouragement.** Remind your child to wash his hands after using the toilet and before meals when he needs reminding. Also, teach your child to cover his mouth when he coughs.

- ✦ **Eat smart.** Talk about healthy foods, and make nutritious meals and snacks together.

- ✦ **Raise a smart chef.** Let your child help plan healthy meals.

- ✦ **Have family fire drills.**

- ✦ **Let him monitor the detector.** Have your child help you change the batteries in the smoke detector.

- ✦ **Do some pre–driver's ed.** Model and talk about safe driving habits when you are in the car.

- ✦ **Buckle up.** As you buckle your seat belt, remind your child to buckle his; don't start driving until everyone's belt is buckled.

- ✦ **Drill bike-helmet safety.** Make sure your child wears a helmet every time he rides his bike. Most serious bike injuries happen when kids don't wear helmets.

- ✦ **Stress safety on the streets.** Continue to practice and talk about pedestrian safety: watching traffic lights, crossing the street at crosswalks, staying on the sidewalk, or facing traffic if you have to walk on the edge of the road.

- ✦ **Raise a substance-free child.** It's not too soon to start mentioning the serious health hazards associated with drugs, smoking, and excessive alcohol use.

Winning Ways to Learn
for 8-Year-Olds

CHAPTER 16

Personal and Social Development

✦

As children continue to learn in school, their confidence and pride in their accomplishments grow as well. Self-confidence continues to be an important component in children's willingness to learn more and tackle new projects.

Children's maturing social skills strengthen their relationships with others and enable them to negotiate more complex situations on their own. This, in turn, reinforces their self-image and allows them to enjoy school and do well in their studies. Children's personal and social development can be seen in their:

Self-concept and self-control

Approach to learning

Interactions with others

SELF-CONCEPT AND SELF-CONTROL

The lives of eight- and nine-year-olds revolve around their peers: They worry about what their friends think of them; they want to do what their friends do, wear what their friends wear, and think like their friends think. Sometimes, this desire for friendship and acceptance challenges their ability to focus on schoolwork or make acceptable choices about behavior. The more confident and capable they feel, the better equipped they are to balance their personal and academic lives. They have an easier time following rules, using materials in appropriate ways, and coping with change. Eight-year-olds want to understand the reasons for particular rules, and they are more likely to obey rules when they have helped make them. They like life to be fairly predictable. However, the more secure their self-image, the easier it is for them to deal with changes as they happen.

FROM SCHOOL TO HOME

Your third-grader has many opportunities to develop her confidence, competence, and comfort in the classroom. She is encouraged and enabled to think of and carry out good ideas—such as a topic for a skit or a creative approach to solving a math problem. She is learning to be responsible about handing in homework on time, doing classroom jobs, or getting classroom work finished. Your eight-year-old is able to find, use, and return classroom materials (computer software, art materials, games, sports equipment). And when she chooses a work partner, shared interest rather than friendship may be the deciding factor. Your child knows how to follow classroom and playground rules, but she has also learned to take a break when things are not going right and even to laugh at small mistakes she makes.

You'll notice a lot of your child's "can-do" attitude at home, too. You may see her work hard to play a musical instrument or improve at a sport. Suddenly she's keeping track of her own daily and weekly schedules, as well as those of family members. She may show increased responsibility when it comes to home tasks, such as taking phone messages or doing chores. When she borrows other family members' materials or belongings, she's now more apt to use them carefully and return them when she's finished than she was last year. Although she may question the need for certain rules, she'll follow them most of the time, and she now has the maturity to adjust to changes in family plans or schedules without becoming upset.

It's Your Turn

To help your eight-year-old's confidence soar:

✦ **Applaud her independent attitude.** Praise your child's efforts to make her own decisions and do things differently from her friends.

✦ **Enjoy your child's uniqueness.** Notice and show appreciation for your child's special qualities and strengths: personality, temperament, intelligence, outlook, talents, skills, sociability, sensitivity, sense of humor, style, and appearance.

✦ **Give her talents free rein.** Encourage her to explore special interests, abilities, and passions, whether they be painting, baseball, cooking, science, music, or writing. In this way you nurture your child's independent spirit and self-worth.

✦ **Get her opinion.** Ask for and consider your child's ideas about household and family issues. This helps her feel that her thoughts really matter.

✦ **And give her useful jobs to do.** Responsibilities that allow her to make a real contribution to your family life, such as cooking dinner and helping to wash the car, will make her feel competent and necessary.

✦ **Let her sharpen her skills.** Have your child help with a task or project that requires a skill she has developed or is of interest to her—for example, writing the shopping list for you or planting a garden.

✦ **Give her some power.** Discuss rules and encourage your child to help create them.

✦ **Let her in on the plan.** Chart family plans together or talk about the next day's schedule at dinner so your child knows what everyone will be doing and when.

✦ **Challenge her responsible self.** Let your child use family materials, equipment, books, and tools, and ask her to treat these things as if they were her own.

✦ **Praise your child's adaptability.** Thank your child for being flexible when plans need to be changed; for your part, try to limit last-minute changes whenever possible.

✦ **Talk about feelings.** Have discussions with your child about behavior and emotions: "How does it make you feel when your friends fight?"; "What do you do when something makes you angry?"

✦ **Compliment her cool.** Praise your child's successful efforts to use self-control in a difficult situation, such as after losing a game or when being teased.

APPROACH TO LEARNING

Third-graders are becoming more independent learners. Some learn best by exploring and doing things; others by watching and listening. Some express their knowledge and ideas best through art, music, or acting; others through talking or writing. They are also becoming more mature learners and can stick with a selected subject for a long time. They're more responsible about choosing what and how they want to learn, and they're willing to try new things, even when they know they may not succeed right away. When they have to make a choice, they are able to consider the pros and cons of each possibility and choose the one they think will work best.

From School to Home

The third-grade classroom offers children interesting learning challenges. Your eight-year-old has the opportunity to share ideas, opinions, and talents with class-mates. He makes choices in learning projects, such as making a list of several ideas for writing a story and choosing the one he thinks will work best. When he chooses a topic for a research project, he is able to collect information in multiple ways, such as reading books, interviewing an expert, and using the Internet. Plus, he's able to sustain work on the project over two or three weeks. Your child will now try increasingly difficult activities, such as a new computer game, and will stick with them even if several tries are needed to achieve success.

You'll see your third-grader show a great deal of interest in a topic over many weeks or months. He may decide to take up a new skill, such as playing a musical instrument, carving wood, or playing a sport, and he'll find a way to learn it from books, a special class, educational television, or a "how-to" video. He'll borrow library books by a particular author or about a particular subject. And he'll make his own decisions about his leisure time. For instance, he may think of a few things to do on a Saturday, consider the advantages and disadvantages of each, and choose one. He may decide to write in a personal journal.

It's Your Turn

Your child's capacity for learning will grow when you:

+ **Acknowledge his new ventures.** Praise your child's willingness to try new things and his desire and ability to see them through.

+ **Ask for his help.** Solicit your child's opinions and suggestions when you need to solve a problem. This will motivate him to reach for new ways to figure things out as well as let him know that you value his competence.

+ **Let him pace himself.** Avoid rushing your child to complete projects, and encourage him to be thorough.

+ **Help your child spend his time.** Guide your child in making wise choices about using free time. For example, suggest that he weed his garden Saturday morning or go to the library today to get the resource book he will need next week.

+ **Model a lust for learning.** Set an example for your child by being a curious learner: Notice and talk about things; read, listen to, and talk about the news; learn a new skill.

+ **Get excited about school.** Show your child that you are interested in his school and his learning. Ask him questions about his school day; look at the work he brings home; help him with homework; go to his school for conferences and special events.

+ **Let him pick out his clothes.** Encourage your child to shop with you for his clothes and make selections. This will enable him to make choices that affect his life, fostering his decision-making ability and his sense of responsibility.

+ **Feed his reading habit.** Provide books (borrowed from the library or school) that you know will be of particular interest to him.

+ **Go places.** Take your child to interesting towns, events, sites, performances, buildings—places that interest you, too.

+ **Join him in a project.** Get involved in a home activity with your child, such as knitting a sweater for your dog, doing a carpentry project, or learning Tai Chi from a videotape. Show him you're open to learning something new, and you'll inspire the learner in him.

INTERACTIONS WITH OTHERS

At this age, children are likely to have one or two very close friends. But being a part of a group is also important to eight-year-olds, so they maintain friendly and cooperative relationships with children who aren't necessarily their best buddies. They work at being a successful group member by taking turns, talking with and complimenting others, making compromises to solve disagreements, and playing fairly. They show increasingly meaningful concern for the feelings of others. All of these behaviors are practiced and reinforced in classes, during sports, or while in after-school care.

Your third-grader values and works at being independent and may not seek out adults as much as she used to. However, when she has trouble resolving a conflict, she is able to ask for suggestions or seek help from adults.

FROM SCHOOL TO HOME

Social interaction is an integral part of a third-grade classroom. To begin with, your child greets her teacher in the morning, discusses things with her during the day, and says goodbye at the end of the day. One-on-one communication happens often with other children, too. For example, your child may congratulate another child for making a good play in a game, or she may make an extra effort to help a class-mate struggling with a disability. She is learning to state her feelings clearly to another child: "I don't think it is fair that you get to use the basketball two days in a row. Can I have a turn?" Your eight-year-old is now likely to bring a problem to a class meeting for discussion. She may also agree to go along with a group decision even when she might prefer not to.

At home and around the neighborhood your child is probably at ease with several children and can play games without lots of arguing about rules. In addition, she knows how to talk politely to adult family friends. It is likely that she enjoys taking part in group activities that involve kids and adults, such as scouts or music groups. Eight-year-olds can feel and express empathy, so it wouldn't be unusual to see your child comfort a sibling or neighborhood child who has been hurt or teased. Negotiation skills are also developing, which enable your child to try to bargain her way out of a conflict: "I'll tell you what, you can use the headphones now if I can have them when I go to bed."

It's Your Turn

To foster your child's interpersonal give-and-take:

✦ **Be mindful of manners.** Teach your child respectful ways to interact with others, such as saying *please* and *thank you*, acknowledging greetings, and so on.

✦ **Provide a social arena.** Support your child's close friendships by helping her arrange out-cf-school time with her pals.

✦ **...and help her expand that arena.** Encourage your child to broaden her friendships beyond her best buddies by helping her plan special events that will include new children.

✦ **Try team spirit.** Involve your child in activities and sports that focus on individual skills as well as team planning, such as swimming, skating, and choral singing.

✦ **Have chats.** Help your child with her conversational skills by talking with her often. The idea is that she practice listening, asking questions, and responding to what you say so she can do these things comfortably with others.

✦ **Let her know she's good with grown-ups.** Praise your child's positive interactions with adult friends, relatives, or neighbors.

✦ **Help her state her case.** Teach your child to express herself with appropriate words in conflict situations: For example, "I don't like it when you boss me around. Please stop!"

✦ **Explore all options.** Brainstorm solutions to real and pretend conflicts so your child can see that there are many possible ways to settle various social issues.

✦ **Encourage her to get over it.** Talk with your child about how to get beyond a fight with someone and go back to being friends. Be sure to ask her how she thinks this can be done.

✦ **Work out publicized issues.** Discuss alternatives to, as well as ways to settle, lawsuits and violence that you hear about on the television news or read about in newspapers.

✦ **Notice character development.** Read books together and discuss how the characters in the story interact with one another and the ways they resolve conflict situations.

CHAPTER 17

Language and Literacy

✦

As they grow older and gain knowledge and skills, children develop increasingly sophisticated abilities in reading, writing, and language. These growing abilities, in turn, reinforce and enhance every other aspect of learning.

Third-graders are more independent in their reading. Their positive attitudes about reading activities and skills (for example, excitement about studying more about their favorite topic, knowing how to use the computer to record their ideas, learning how the Internet can enhance their interest in science) continue to be crucial to their success in learning in all areas. Third-graders' progress in language and literacy can be seen in three areas:

Listening and speaking

Literature and reading

Writing and spelling

LISTENING AND SPEAKING

For eight-year-olds, listening and speaking are closely connected. Children listen to hear ideas, get information, follow directions, and be entertained. As they listen, they think about what they hear and often ask specific questions to clear up confusion or expand their knowledge. Generally, third-graders speak clearly. Depending on the situation, they use different tones of voice and different volumes—loud, soft, or moderate. They continue to expand their vocabulary and can describe objects, events, and places thoroughly and accurately. They also change how they speak based on whether they're trying to persuade, inform, entertain, give directions, express an opinion, or share feelings.

From School to Home

Your third-grader's teacher and class offer him a wealth of language-building opportunities. For example, he listens to the directions for a computer program and follows them step-by-step. He listens to a visiting artist talk about her work and may then use some of the techniques himself. He may also listen and take notes as a classmate or visitor makes a presentation, ask follow-up questions, and then write a brief report. On the verbal side of language, he speaks clearly, looks at his audience of classmates, and uses pauses and gestures to express his ideas or opinions. He explains to a small group of students how he solved a math problem. He gives convincing arguments in a debate or discussion.

Of course, listening and speaking are also a big part of his home activities. He'll listen to: music or books on tape for pleasure; a series of directions and then follow them without reminders; radio or television and then explain what he learned. Your child is able to give detailed descriptions of events that happen in school and can actively participate in family conversations. He'll use convincing words when asking for something or when explaining why he did something the way he did.

It's Your Turn

To sharpen your child's language skills:

+ **Listen!** Listen to and talk with your child. Children need an audience in order to learn to speak well.

+ **...and show *him* how to listen.** Model good listening skills when having conversations with your child: Keep your focus on him, show your interest, and really listen to his words.

+ **Ask his opinion.** Make sure your child gets a chance to express his thoughts during family discussions and conversations.

+ **Let him speak for himself**–in public situations, such as at the doctor's office or when someone talks to him while standing in line at the store.

+ **Keep reading to him.** He's not too old for you to read aloud to him and discuss what you have read.

+ **...and read all kinds of things.** Different kinds of books will help your child hear how language is used in different ways.

+ **Lay it all out up front.** Give complete directions for a project or task at the beginning instead of giving them step-by-step along the way. Your child is mature enough to listen to and remember them without reminders.

+ **Play music.** Set aside time for listening to CDs, tapes, or the radio together.

+ **Discuss the sounds of music.** Talk to your child about the music he listens to. Ask him to tell you about the voices, the instruments, and the words.

+ **Let him make noise.** Encourage your child to experiment with sound effects using objects around the home. For example, listen to the rain on the porch roof or dripping from the rain spout. "How could we make a sound like that using our hands or our voice?"

+ **Play games.** Word games can expand your child's verbal ability. For example, "Twenty Questions" will help your child learn how–to–what else?–ask good questions.

+ **Have him act it out.** Encourage your child to perform skits and puppet shows of familiar or original stories. This will serve to increase his improvisational word power.

LITERATURE AND READING

Most third-graders enjoy reading and are good at it. They can pick up almost any printed matter, read it (whether for pleasure or to get information), and understand it. They use many reading strategies—phonetically sounding out words, looking at pictures for clues, reading ahead and then coming back to a difficult word, memorizing, responding to initial letter sounds—almost automatically. Third-graders are capable of reading books that present complicated words, stories, and ideas. Talking, writing, or creating art projects about the books they read helps them understand the purpose, characters, action, and setting of the stories. Many eight-year-olds have developed their own tastes for certain types of books or for books written by particular authors.

FROM SCHOOL TO HOME

Your third-grade teacher provides literacy materials and encourages your child to read many different kinds of texts, such as short stories, poetry, computer instructions, and game directions. Your child gains reading skills from a variety of experiences. While reading, your child learns to correct her own mistakes. With other children, she may have the opportunity to put on a small skit, acting out the main character in a story she's read. She may also write a review of a book, explaining the book's strengths and weaknesses. She may have the opportunity in school to listen to another student read and help the other child recognize words or understand the content.

At home your child reads for pleasure or to get information without being prompted. She probably wants to read before going to sleep, and she enjoys reading to younger siblings or other young children. She'll likely ask you how to pronounce hard-to-read words and discuss their meaning. And she'll want to go to the library to look for a book written by an author she has read about in school.

"I use this book as a reference, rereading specific areas to give me ideas of what to do for my child."

It's Your Turn

Reading has played and will continue to play a key role in your child's learning success. To nurture her lifelong love of reading:

+ **Surround her with books.** Make sure your child has plenty of interesting books to read: Borrow them from the library or friends; buy them at a discount on the Web or from second-hand bookstores or yard sales.

+ **Read what she reads.** Pore over some of your child's books and have book talks together.

+ **Have her read aloud**—to younger siblings or other children and to you.

+ **Trade off chapters.** Share the reading of a book aloud by alternating pages or chapters with your child.

+ **Make a tape.** Record your child reading a favorite book aloud, and send tapes to grandparents or other interested relatives.

+ **Query your child.** Ask questions about the books she has read: For example, "Where does the story take place? What is the main character like? What happens to the characters in this book? Why did a character make certain choices and what might have happened had different choices been made?"

+ **Ask pros for advice.** Ask librarians or bookstore owners to suggest new titles or authors your child might enjoy.

+ **Meet the authors.** Keep an eye out for opportunities to meet or attend sessions led by children's book authors.

+ **Introduce the classics.** They might not be your child's first choice, but you can open her mind to great literature by talking about your favorite classics. Occasionally read aloud to your child from great books.

+ **To each her own, together.** Have a regular reading time, maybe after dinner, when you and your child each read your own book. Doing this will reinforce your child's independent enjoyment of books.

+ **Have her try chain reading.** Encourage your child to become interested in a series of books, such as the Animorphs or Dear America series.

+ **Be a subscriber.** Subscribe to a children's magazine (ask your librarian for suggestions), and try out some of the activities together. Encourage your child to read the stories or news articles and then tell you what they are about.

WRITING AND SPELLING

Third-graders know that writing is a way to say what they think, tell what they know, and entertain others. They know a lot about writing (when to use capital letters, which punctuation marks to use and when to use them, how to use quotation marks), but they still need to be reminded to use these rules. Eight-year-olds know how to plan before writing and later to read the final work, fixing mistakes and making the writing clearer if necessary. Their finished drafts will be legible and fairly well organized and should make sense.

By now your child uses standard, correct spelling for the words he writes frequently. He may still use some invented or temporary spelling for words that are new to him. He is learning how to use a student dictionary and perhaps a computer spell-check.

FROM SCHOOL TO HOME

In school your child writes a variety of material, such as stories, reports, poems, plays, letters, and signs. He makes a plan or outline for a report, writes it, and may have a classmate review it to make sure it is correct and clear. He uses periods, exclamation points, question marks, commas, and quotation marks in his writing. He may write one or two drafts of a story or report, make corrections, additions, and deletions, and then type the final version on the computer. He uses a student dictionary to check spellings of unfamiliar words, and he may run a spell-check before printing out a computer-processed piece of writing.

Most likely, you see your child do a lot of writing at home, as well. He writes notes, cards, and letters with organized sentences to family members and friends. He knows to use capital letters for the first letter of the first word of a sentence, for the word I, and for the first letter in names. He may write about daily events in a journal, diary, or family log book. Your child will ask you to check his homework for spelling mistakes, and he'll use a dictionary to check the spelling of a difficult word.

It's Your Turn

Your child will continue to build writing and spelling skills when you:

+ **Stock up on supplies.** Keep plenty of paper, pencils, and pens handy for your child to write with.

+ **Suggest that he write every day.** Don't push. Encourage, and make it fun by proposing fun or interesting topics or projects. Let him know the writing doesn't have to be long.

+ **Go over his work with him.** Read your child's writing and help him fix obvious mistakes.

+ **Share wonderful words**–by pointing out writing that you think is special in some way. Begin by saying, for instance, "Listen to how this author describes the ocean."

+ **Write together.** Pen funny stories with your child, taking turns writing sentences.

+ **Encourage correspondence.** Suggest that your child write letters to the newspaper, relatives, pen pals, friends, and so on.

+ **Use writing at home.** Ask your child to do some of the household writing, such as signs, notes, instructions, shopping lists, and reminders.

+ **Play word games**–word scrambles, "Scrabble," "Boggle," and the like.

+ **Have family spelling bees.** Remember to keep it fun and light so the competition doesn't bog down the progress.

+ **Let him look it up.** Get a student dictionary for your child, or help him use a regular dictionary.

+ **Teach him some tricks.** Explain some of the methods that helped you learn to spell certain words as a child, such as the way you memorized certain spelling rules or idioms.

+ **Solve word puzzles together.** Crosswords, word searches, and Jumbles are fun, and they help with spelling.

+ **Drill with your child.** Help him with his weekly spelling words from school by using flash cards, playing "Hang Man," making up anagrams, and so on.

+ **Show off his work.** Display your child's writing on the refrigerator, just like you used to display his artwork when he was younger.

CHAPTER 18

Mathematical Thinking

✦

Eight-year-olds are learning new arithmetic skills that will help them to become more confident in mathematics and that will enable them to understand more abstract numerical and algebraic problems. They also learn to use their insights into mathematical principles to identify relationships among objects and quantities and to find increasingly creative approaches to problem solving. These skills contribute in important ways to the development of children's critical thinking skills. Children's progress in mathematical thinking is seen in four areas:

> **Patterns and relationships**
>
> **Numbers and their use**
>
> **Geometry, spatial relations,**
> **and measurement**
>
> **Probability and statistics**

PATTERNS AND RELATIONSHIPS

Third-graders can create original patterns and extend patterns that someone else has started. They can use words to describe complex patterns of actions, objects, and numbers. They can also use the patterns they see to make predictions, draw conclusions, and solve problems: For example, they can look at the pattern 36, 32, 28, 24... and predict that the next number will be 20, because they see that each number is 4 less than the previous one. Later on, these kinds of patterns will help your child solve algebraic equations like: If X - 4 = 12, then X =__.

For your eight-year-old, understanding mathematical relationships means looking at a large set of objects and deciding how to sort the set into smaller groups, for example, sorting a group of shells by size or shape. And now she is able to deal with overlapping groups, for example, sorting pieces of fabric into striped, dotted, and plaid groups, then creating an overlapping group that has both stripes and dots.

FROM SCHOOL TO HOME

In her third-grade classroom, your child has many opportunities to work with patterns. She finds different ways to sort the class into smaller groups: by age, gender, height, weight, hair color, eye color, family size, shoe size, and so on. She gets the chance to extend number patterns, such as 2, 4, 8, 16, 32... She may sort a group of animal pictures into sets according to different criteria, such as habitat and size. She may create intricate patterns on paper and then reproduce them with yarn as a weaving. More and more she'll recognize patterns in everyday life: in phone numbers, in musical passages, in the seasons, and in the way living things grow.

She'll also discover and notice life patterns around her home environment, such as in leaves, flowers, tire treads, clothing, and wallpaper. She'll find many different ways to sort a collection of cards, shells, or rocks. And you'll see her arrange her books in different ways: alphabetically, by author, by size, or by topic. She may create pattern borders around drawings or a complex pattern with beads for a necklace.

It's Your Turn

To further your child's pattern perception:

+ **Go on a road hunt.** Any time you're in the car for a while, challenge your child to look for various patterns—in signs, street markings, buildings, walls, fences, groups of vehicles, and so on. Together, describe in words how the patterns are formed.

+ **...and on a nature hunt.** Suggest that she also look for patterns in nature: in flower petals, leaves, shells, clouds, dried-earth cracks, spider webs, and so on.

+ **Listen for patterns.** Together, find repeating patterns in songs, poems, and chants.

+ **Offer her the creative-pattern challenge:** Invite your child to sort a large group of objects, such as shape blocks, buttons, or a collection of leaves or stones, using a sorting rule that will be hard for you to guess.

+ **Put her on sorting duty.** Ask her to sort laundry, coins, groceries, utensils, tools.

+ **Let her sift through junk.** Give your child the job of sorting and organizing a junk drawer in your kitchen or home office.

+ **Give her a grid.** Supply your child with plenty of graph paper on which to make pattern designs.

+ **Get into home design.** Create patterns with your child to use as borders for letters, place mats, or photo frames.

+ **Let your child be a food stylist.** Ask her to arrange crackers or raw vegetables for a dip on a tray; suggest that she be creative and come up with an interesting pattern.

+ **Sort out her room.** Help your child organize her toys into categories, such as puzzles, stuffed animals, science materials, games, and sports equipment, for easy access.

+ **...and her books.** Help her arrange her books by topics, authors, or their use (information, mysteries, poetry, and so on).

+ **Discuss jigsaw strategies.** Assemble puzzles together and talk about the different clues you use to fit pieces together.

NUMBERS AND THEIR USE

Math is an ever-growing part of children's learning life. The way third-graders solve number problems is increasingly systematic and organized. They know several strategies, such as using trial and error (guessing and checking), making a drawing, creating a diagram or chart to show solutions to problems, adding and subtracting in their heads, and counting backwards by 2s, 5s, and 10s.

Your child builds on what he has learned about numbers in earlier grades. He is able to count and write numbers, compare larger and larger numbers, use different strategies for adding and subtracting numbers, understand the place values in numbers, make good estimates with larger and larger amounts, understand and learn multiplication facts, and learn how to read, write, and compare fractions.

FROM SCHOOL TO HOME

At school your child adds and subtracts in many situations, such as when buying items from the school store and adding up the weights of items. He uses objects to help him learn to add three separate 3-digit numbers. He may use blocks to help him find out how many ways 30 people can be divided into equal-sized groups. Or he might divide a pretend pizza into halves, thirds, fourths, sixths, and eighths, labeling the pieces and writing the fractions in order from smallest to largest. Your eight-year-old reads, writes, and compares large numbers every day in class, and he works with a group to compare strategies for solving word problems.

Your child will bring his math skills home, for instance, to keep track of who won, who came in second, and who came in third in a game. He'll make good estimates of how much something weighs, how much a container will hold, or how many people are in a large group. Perhaps he'll ask you for, say, $5.75 to add to $6.25, with which he'll pay for a soccer ball that costs $12.00. He may also ask you to cut a pie into 6 pieces instead of 8, explaining that "Sixths are bigger than eighths, so we'll get bigger pieces of pie that way!"

"It's great to focus on the fact that there's more to math than addition, subtraction, multiplication, and division."

It's Your Turn

Count on your child to know his numbers when you:

+ **Play a numbers game.** Ask him to read multiple-digit numbers in newspapers, on buildings, and in books.

+ **Have him solve life's problems.** Ask your child to help with math issues that come up: For example, "A pizza comes with 8 slices. Your 4 friends will eat 3 slices each. How many pizzas should we order?"

+ **Let him "guesstimate."** Ask your child to estimate, for example, how many books will fit in his backpack or how many people are attending a concert.

+ **Challenge him to challenge you.** Encourage your child to make up word problems for you to solve. He might ask you, for example, "Guess how many crayons are in my box?"; "Guess how many weeks of allowance I need to buy that new model car we saw?"

+ **Be smart shoppers together.** Give your child problems to solve at the market: "How much do you think this food will cost? How many pounds of hamburger can we get for $5.00?"

+ **Let him keep score.** Play games and put your child in charge of adding up the points.

+ **Query his answers.** When your child solves a math problem, ask him how he figured it out.

+ **Play with the piggy bank.** Using a collection of loose change, ask your child questions, such as, "How many ways can you make $1.36? How much do you have in nickels? dimes? quarters? How much do you have if you just count the quarters and pennies?"

+ **Play the phone-book math challenge.** For example, ask, "Find a phone number in which the digits add up to 37"; "Add the individual numbers in these three phone numbers."

+ **Have him work all the angles.** Give your child a number—18, for example—and have him come up with as many ways as possible to arrive at that number: 9 + 9, 20 - 2, 6 x 3, 36 ÷ 2.

GEOMETRY, SPATIAL RELATIONS, AND MEASUREMENT

By the time they reach third grade, children have learned what happens when shapes are combined with other shapes or broken down into smaller shapes. They can compare two-dimensional and three-dimensional shapes (circles and spheres, squares and cubes). They solve problems with shapes, such as substituting one shape for another in a design, making a mirror image of a design, making a symmetrical design from an odd number of blocks, or finding out how many blocks of one shape fit into another shape.

An eight-year-old's understanding of measurement—height, weight, and length—is expanding to include speed, temperature, volume, and time. She understands why it is important to use standard units, such as inches, pounds, gallons, and hours. She can now read measurements that fall between whole numbers, such as a quarter-inch, a half-degree, and so on.

FROM SCHOOL TO HOME

The third-grade classroom offers all kinds of geometric, spatial, and measurement challenges. Your child copies, creates, measures, and describes various shapes; she talks about the number of sides and angles. She may solve spatial problems by predicting and finding out how many blocks of one shape will fit into another shape. She'll weigh objects and compare the weights: "The red car weighs 7 ounces more than the green one." On the computer, she may create symmetrical designs using a geometry program. She may also take indoor- and outdoor-temperature readings and compare them.

At home your eight-year-old will use shape names to describe things around her: "My friend at school has a new watch shaped like a hexagon." She'll also use the shape names to describe things she does: "First you fold the square in half so you have two triangles. Then you fold it in half again so that you can see four triangles." She may build complex structures using blocks, folded paper, or assorted recycled materials. She's able to measure a space in her bedroom to see if a piece of furniture will fit into it. In your garden, she can figure out how many rows of peas will fit if the rows are 18 inches apart.

IT'S YOUR TURN

Learning keeps shaping up for your child as you:

+ **Chat about shape-making.** Let your child work with construction toys or geometry puzzles, and encourage her to talk about what she is doing as she works.

+ **Let things take shape on paper.** Challenge your child to draw multi-shaped designs with a ruler and a compass.

+ **Have a quilting bee.** Help your child make a small quilt by cutting out triangles, squares, and rectangles and sewing them together in patterns.

+ **Practice origami.** Get a book on origami from the library to learn together how to fashion these wonderful shapes from paper.

+ **Play with homemade "Tinkertoys."** Offer your child toothpicks and clay (or small marshmallows) to build designs or a simple bridge or building. Talk about the shapes in the structures when they are finished.

+ **Have her shape art.** Let your child cut shapes from paper and put them together to form pictures.

+ **Talk measurements.** Spur her to think in terms of measuring words by asking questions, such as: "How long did it take the bus to get to school today?"; "How much do you think the rock weighs?"

+ **...and read measurements.** Ask your child to read a thermometer, ruler, scale, or measuring cup.

+ **Let her watch the clock.** Help your child learn to tell time by looking at a clock with hands and reporting the time she starts to get dressed, eat breakfast, or make her bed and, when finished, figuring out how long it has taken to do each activity.

+ **Have her stay on schedule.** Suggest to your child that she keep her own calendar on which to note important dates.

+ **Keep a growth chart.** Help your child keep an ongoing graph of her height and weight.

+ **Map it out with her.** Show your child how to use a scale on a map to figure out how many miles it is to a destination.

PROBABILITY AND STATISTICS

For third-graders, work with probability and statistics involves collecting and organizing data to make it easier to understand. It also involves using this information to make predictions. How do children do this? They collect data using surveys, score cards, tally sheets, or lists. They organize the data on graphs and charts. They also learn to read graphs and charts that other people have made and to make predictions based on those graphs or charts. For example, by looking at temperature graphs from past years for the month of June, they can predict what kinds of clothing they should take on the June 6 field trip.

FROM SCHOOL TO HOME

In school your eight-year-old compiles and uses data in fun and interesting ways. He might take a school survey of favorite sports and make a chart of this data for the school's front hall. Perhaps he'll read a tally that shows how many times a team has won and lost, then make a prediction about the outcome of the next game. He could be asked to measure and record the growth of a plant for six weeks, then make a graph to show its growth. He might make a chart to record how many times a 6 comes up in 30 rolls of a die or learn how to make simple line, bar, or pie graphs on a computer.

He'll use these kinds of skills at home, too, as he makes a chart to keep track of how much money is in his piggy bank or monitors how much time it takes to do homework and then makes a bar graph to show his teacher. Your child can now read the weather maps and charts in the newspaper or on television. And, just for fun, he might keep a chart over time showing wins and losses for family members in a favorite card game.

"We both enjoyed the phone-book activity. We came up with different answers but we were both always right!"

It's Your Turn

To help nurture your child's statistical skills:

+ **Tell him to keep track.** Encourage your child to collect and organize data, such as sports scores or the types of birds seen at the feeder.

+ **Make the media matter.** Teach your child how to look for and understand interesting graphs and charts in the newspaper, and ask him to try to find two or three from every Sunday paper that you can talk about.

+ **Help him manage his money.** Together, make a chart or graph that shows how your child spends his allowance each week in categories like food, books, savings, games, and so on.

+ **Keep track of the family.** Make charts or graphs that show each family member's daily activities and household jobs in terms of the amount of time spent doing them.

+ **Foster botanical interests.** Help your child graph the comparative growth of different plants in the garden or different bulbs in pots.

+ **Practice meal planning.** Chart with your child the family menus for a week; then chart the food groups included or the vitamins provided in a week.

+ **Throw the dice.** Make guesses about, for example, how many 8s you will throw in 50 dice rolls.

+ **Conduct statistical interviews.** Have your child survey family members on a variety of questions—their favorite season of the year, favorite sport, favorite flavor of ice cream—and then graph the results.

+ **Play meteorologist.** Set up a bar graph with your child to record daily temperatures over the next three months. If you don't have an outdoor thermometer, get the temperature from the newspaper or the Weather Channel.

+ **Track books.** Have your child keep a tally of the number of books he reads over a two-month period in categories such as sports, mystery novels, natural history, reference, and so on. Be sure to talk about the graph when it is finished.

CHAPTER 19

Scientific Thinking

✦

Eight-year-olds can be expected to observe objects closely, notice details, begin documenting their discoveries, and draw their own conclusions. They are becoming adept at using both the practical tools of science (thermometers, microscopes, balance scales) and the conceptual scientific method. Their growing scientific skills are seen in the areas of:

Observing, investigating, and questioning

Predicting, explaining, and forming conclusions

OBSERVING, INVESTIGATING, AND QUESTIONING

Third-graders have developed the skills and patience to observe things closely. As young scientists, they use their senses and special tools to learn all they can about an object or event. Their observations raise questions in their minds, which they then try to answer by setting up experiments or investigations. They know that certain tools can help them observe and gather more information. As eight-year-olds observe the way things are alike or different, make comparisons, and categorize things, they are spurred to ask increasingly specific questions. Their questions lead to collecting things, organizing data, and testing or experimenting to find answers.

FROM SCHOOL TO HOME

In the third-grade classroom, students have ample opportunity for observation and discovery. Your child sets up observational experiments, such as growing plants under varying conditions to find out which cause them to thrive. She uses scientific tools to help her observe more carefully, using a microscope, for example, to compare a strand of human hair and a strand of a dog's hair. She asks questions before beginning an investigation, such as, "Which type of soap works best to make bubbles?" or, "Can one bubble be inside another?" Over time she may observe a classroom pet to learn its eating habits. Or she'll work at a water table, testing various substances' resistance to erosion, and she'll wonder, "What would happen if we combined clay and sand?"

At home you'll see your child show interest in animals, birds, insects, stars, or other natural wonders and seek information about them. Perhaps she'll find an earthworm and put it in a jar with soil to find out how it digs tunnels. Watch as she uses a magnifying glass to observe minute things or a kitchen scale to weigh a variety of items. She may make detailed drawings of things she observes, such as a flower, a seed, or the bark of a tree. And she'll ask ever more challenging questions about how things work, such as, "Why does food in a microwave cook so fast?"; "What would happen if we burned all the trash instead of taking it to the dump?"

IT'S YOUR TURN

To bring out the scientist in your third-grader:

✦ **Ask her to sense and describe:** Encourage your child's natural curiosity by reminding her to look, listen, smell, and touch and then to describe what her senses tell her.

✦ **Illustrate science.** Make scientific drawings with your child, depicting, for example, seeds growing (illustrating each stage of development–stalk, leaves, bud, blossom) or what your finger looks like through a magnifying glass.

✦ **Equip her.** Let your child use science tools–a magnifying glass, a thermometer, a scale–to explore, test, and measure items in and around the house.

✦ **Let her loose in the "lab."** Help your child set up experiments to test out ideas: For instance, when she says, "I think cold water freezes faster than hot water," let her use the freezer and an ice-cube tray to test the theory.

✦ **Bring out the ornithologist in her.** Set up a bird-feeding station, borrow a bird identification book from the library, and encourage your child to observe and describe how different birds look and behave.

✦ **...and the meteorologist in her.** Follow the weather together: Keep charts of temperatures and weather conditions, and listen to weather forecasts.

✦ **...and the stargazer.** With a book on stars and planets, look at your own sky; together identify specific constellations, or chart the path and shape of the moon over a month's time.

✦ **Go buggy!** Capture insects to study for a day or two, and then let them go.

✦ **Find a tree of knowledge.** Pick out a neighborhood tree, find out what kind it is, read about it in a tree book, sketch it in different seasons, do bark rubbings, and collect its leaves and press them.

✦ **Explore with your child.** Help her find answers to questions about life and nature; let her know when you don't know the answers so you can discover them together.

✦ **Inspire her questions with your questions.** Set an example by asking probing questions, such as, "What would happen if...?"or, "How could we find out about...?"

✦ **Play "20 Science Questions":** "I'm thinking of an animal. You can ask 20 questions to try to figure out which animal it is."

PREDICTING, EXPLAINING, AND FORMING CONCLUSIONS

By the time children are in the third grade they are beginning to answer questions based on things they have observed or learned from books. When they predict answers, they now look for a pattern or clue from what they already know. For example, in reference to what frogs eat, eight-year-olds would think about where frogs live and predict that their food comes from a pond. Children this age can communicate their scientific knowledge by talking, writing, drawing, and making charts or graphs.

From School to Home

In school your child is learning to participate in all kinds of scientific processes. He makes predictions before observing: For example, he will make a list of what might be found in a pail of pond water before looking at the water with a magnifying glass. He can explain differences observed in an experiment: He'll watch what happens when a candle is placed in different parts of the classroom and try to explain the differences in the way it burns. He's able to predict what will happen during various stages of a process, such as a cooking project. And he makes observations over time and gives explanations for the patterns he notices: For example, he'll study the classroom hamster and give explanations about why it is more active on cloudy days than on sunny days. He can now answer complicated questions—such as, "Why did you do it that way?"—with clear descriptions of how each step in an experiment led to the next.

He'll then come home and tell you about an experiment he did at school, describing what he's learned. Around the house you may see your eight-year-old watch the behavior of ants on the sidewalk and then draw a picture to show what he saw. Or he may make predictions about the next day's weather based on the night sky. He's able to conclude that since the seeds in the garden have been in the ground for a week now, maybe they will show green sprouts in the morning. He'll try to answer a younger child's science questions, such as, "Why do the leaves turn red in the fall?"

IT'S YOUR TURN

You encourage your child's predicting and problem-solving when you :

+ **Query his predictions:** Ask your child to explain, "Why do you think that will happen?"; "What do you think now that you know more about that?"; "How do you know that?"

+ **If it's sketchy, have him sketch it.** Suggest that your child draw a picture if he is having trouble explaining something with words.

+ **Hit the books.** Take your child to the library and borrow a book that explains scientific phenomena, such as *The Way Things Work* by David MacAulay.

+ **Honor his theories.** Show respect for your child's predictions even when they appear to be wild guesses.

+ **Listen!** Show interest in your child's scientific explanations and conclusions.

+ **Spark wonderment.** Encourage your child to think about the world around him by, for example, suggesting he focus on animal behavior and asking him, "Did you ever wonder how animals know it's time to come out of hibernation?"

+ **Have him explore reference options.** Suggest that he use various resources to answer questions and explain phenomena—encyclopedias, the Internet, guide books, an expert or professional, and so on.

+ **Let him guess first.** Encourage your child to make guesses or predictions about his questions before you help him find answers and explanations.

+ **Muse about machinery.** Wonder with your child about how mechanical things work: "What happens in a car when we put on the brakes?"; "What makes the heavy airplane lift off into the sky?"

+ **Find a shared interest.** Focus on an intriguing science topic with your child, such as the study of stars or the mechanics of hurricanes or tornadoes.

CHAPTER 20

Social Studies

✦

The focus for third-graders' social studies continues to be on themselves, their families, and their communities. In addition, there is likely to be more attention given to different peoples and their traditions. Third-graders learn more about how climate and geography affect the way people live and work, how history shapes their lives, and how customs vary from one culture to another. Eight-year-olds study about their world in two areas:

People and how they live their lives

How the past, the land, and people affect one another

PEOPLE AND HOW THEY LIVE THEIR LIVES

Third-graders know that people around the world are the same in some ways and very different in other ways. They can think about physical characteristics, feelings, and life-styles of different people. They increasingly understand how people depend on each other for goods (clothing, food, tools, and household items) and for services (fire and police protection, medical and dental care, and personal services, such as dry cleaning, hair cuts, and trash collection).

Third-graders are also learning that rules and leaders help groups of people live together comfortably and safely. As they talk about school rules, they come to understand that rules and laws help insure that everyone is treated fairly. They have seen how rules are made in the school community and are now ready to understand how local government works, how leaders are chosen, and how rules become laws.

FROM SCHOOL TO HOME

In school an eight-year-old learns about the language, food, family types, dress, and celebrations of another culture and may enact this information in a play. A class assignment might be to interview a person from another country and write a report that compares that person's life with her own. With classmates your child may set up a cooperative project, such as a newspaper, in which everyone has a specific job to perform. Also in class she'll have the opportunity to listen to people who have different jobs and then write about how those people help others, what type of training they have, and what things they like (or dislike) about their jobs. She'll learn about school and community rules and then may debate the pros and cons of a particular law or rule, such as a leash law, school dress-code, or seat-belt law.

Your child may come home one day and discuss something she learned in school about another culture: "Did you know that in China more people ride bicycles than drive cars?" She may make drawings that show people and lifestyles different from her own, such as a person in a wheelchair, or people with different skin colors or different style houses. She'll likely ask you and other adults about your jobs or about other jobs you might describe. Suddenly she's talking about the rules she would make if she were the mayor or town manager.

It's Your Turn

To expand her appreciation of others:

✦ **Focus on friendships.** Talk about what makes the people your child knows special and unique and different from herself.

✦ **Broaden her book sense.** Go to the library to borrow books that tell about people from other countries.

✦ **Be international–culture vultures.** Look at art or listen to music from different parts of the world.

✦ **Voice respect for variety.** Through the openness of your behavior, words, and actions, help your child appreciate human differences rather than fear them, as well as respect people who look or act differently.

✦ **Diversify TV viewing.** Watch and discuss with your child television programs about people who are different from your family.

✦ **Talk politics.** Discuss the pros and cons of local government issues.

✦ **Teach appreciation**–for individuals who help your family, such as the police officer who patrols your neighborhood, the gas station attendant, the trash collector, and those you may never meet who perform services your family depends upon, such as farmers and utility workers.

✦ **Take your child to work.** Show her what you do, what tools or machines you use, and how you work together with other people.

✦ **Do occupational research.** Read books with your child about different kinds of work.

✦ **Introduce fiscal responsibility.** Talk to your child about the cost of goods and services, and discuss what a budget is and how it works.

✦ **Praise your child's social skills.** Compliment her for being a good leader when she helps somebody solve a problem.

✦ **Let her help.** Assist your child in arranging to do occasional odd jobs for an elderly or disabled person. In this way you encourage her to be a caring member of society.

HOW THE PAST, THE LAND, AND PEOPLE AFFECT ONE ANOTHER

For third-graders history is very personal. They learn the history of their own families and their community by talking with older people, looking at old photographs, studying old buildings, and visiting museums.

They learn about geography by reading, studying, and making maps. Through reading and discussions they learn how people change the environment by building highways, constructing building complexes, dumping garbage in the ocean, or damming up rivers. Children also learn about how the environment, geography, and climate affect people's food, housing, transportation, and jobs.

FROM SCHOOL TO HOME

In class, your eight-year-old learns about his personal history, perhaps by making a timeline of his life with photographs and words. He studies other histories, too, such as the history of machines (telephone, computer, television) from their earliest days to the present. Plus he identifies ways people's lives have been changed by these machines. Your child may study the history of a local river—learning how it has affected people and how people have affected it—as a way of understanding changes in the relationship between land and people. He realizes the effects of climate and environment on lifestyles by making a display of houses found in very different locations around the world. Further knowledge of his world comes from making maps—both two- and three-dimensional—of the local community, complete with streets and buildings.

He'll want more information about his past from his home environment. So he'll want to look at old photographs of you, grandparents, and great-grandparents. He'll try to imagine what life was like before modern conveniences, such as running water, electricity, or cars; he may ask, "What did people do at night before there were lights and television?" He'll be curious about technology, how the Internet works, what life was like before telephones, how machines are made in factories. And he might think about how life would be different if your family lived somewhere else: for example, "If we lived in the city we probably wouldn't drive the car so much." Finally, don't be surprised when his appreciation of the environment spurs him to remind family members to recycle.

IT'S YOUR TURN

You'll encourage his understanding of history and life today when you:

+ **Seek out the past.** Visit a history museum together, and write a story about the "olden days."

+ **Get historical.** Help your child think up questions to ask grandparents or older neighbors about how their lives were different 50 years ago.

+ **Have him question *his* past.** Have him question some family members about what life was like when he was 2 or 3 years old.

+ **Go back.** Share family photo albums and talk about people, places, and events of the past.

+ **Let him shape his life.** Help your child make a photo album or scrapbook of his own life.

+ **Check out historical fiction.** Read children's historical books—such as the Dear America or My Name Is America series books (Scholastic)—and talk about the differences between then and now.

+ **Take turns telling "then-and-now" stories:** Trade off tales with your child: "Then I couldn't pronounce big words and now I can" (him); "Then we listened to the radio and now we watch TV" (you).

+ **Go back again.** Occasionally make a point of doing things the old-fashioned way: Cook over a fire; use kerosene lanterns or candles; make your own music instead of listening to the stereo.

+ **Find it on the map.** Have him look up where you're going on vacation or where a relative lives.

+ **Get seasonal.** Ask your child to help you prepare for changing weather or seasons: Batten down for a hurricane or blizzard; put on storm windows or snow tires; maintain fans and air conditioners.

+ **Get into nature shows.** Watch television programs about the environment or geography, and talk about how people live differently around the world.

+ **Become environmental.** Participate together in family or community projects to improve the environment: recycling, gardening, Earth Day projects.

+ **Go international.** Watch television or find Internet sites about people, the environment, and geography of different places all over the world. Talk about how things are different from the part of the world you live in.

CHAPTER 21

The Arts

✦

Artistic expression and creativity are very important in the lives of third-graders. The arts give them important ways to communicate and nearly limitless ways to develop their creativity. As their physical dexterity grows, so do the options for artistic expression. As they become more expressive and creative, they also become better able to understand and value the creative works of others. Third-graders' education in the arts can be seen in two areas:

Artistic expression

Artistic appreciation

ARTISTIC EXPRESSION

Artistic expression is a way of letting other people know what you think about or how you feel. By the time children are in third grade, they can create well-organized, detailed works of art to express their ideas, experiences, and emotions. They are creative in their use of artistic materials. They use familiar materials in new ways; they combine materials to get a new effect; and they make multiple attempts to get their art production just right.

FROM SCHOOL TO HOME

Certainly art is practiced for art's sake in the classroom. But creative expression is also used as a method for study. Your child may mix many shades of green when painting a forest mural for a science project, for example. Or she'll design, build, and display a model of an original house as part of a study of buildings and architecture. Your child will use more than one art form to express herself: She might draw a self portrait and then make a three-dimensional self portrait out of clay. She'll combine art with other forms of communication by writing a story and then acting it out with body movements, scenery, and music. In addition, she may create specific types of poetry, such as haiku.

Her creativity shines at home, too. Your eight-year-old may use furniture, blankets, and household items in imaginative ways to set the stage for dramatizing a story or creating a dance show. She'll combine crayons and markers to get interesting effects when drawing; she'll use recycled materials with odd bits of paper, glue, and scissors to make a collage that depicts a story or expresses a feeling. She's likely to create a special drawing to send to a grandparent. And she'll make up songs while on a long car trip.

"We like the activity in which you put your child's art in frames and display it. My son drew a picture of himself playing. Then we made a frame with glue, stickers, pens, and paper cut into different shapes. We really enjoyed it."

IT'S YOUR TURN

To encourage and promote your child's creative instincts:

✦ **Keep art supplies on hand**–different kinds and sizes of paper, foil, scissors, a stapler, a hole-puncher, markers, crayons, pens, pencils, glue, and Scotch tape–to make sure your child always has tools for creative expression.

✦ **Be Picassos together.** Find time to create works of art *with* your child.

✦ **Show it off.** To let her know that you appreciate her creative endeavors, put some of your child's artwork in frames and display it in a prominent place.

✦ **Be her audience**–and enjoy her musical or dramatic productions.

✦ **Commend her creative thinking.** Notice your child's thoughtful solutions to problems; say, for instance, "You were very clever to think of using crumpled wax paper to get that sound effect."

✦ **Inspire her with junk.** Start a collection of "beautiful junk" that she can use for art projects–found material, such as bits of yarn, small pieces of felt, string, bits of fabric, straws, Popsicle sticks, empty egg cartons, glue, glitter, buttons, outgrown socks (for making puppets or a doll), seeds, leaves, pine cones, sticks, twigs, and so on.

✦ **Write a song together.** Make up words to music that tell a story about things your family does.

✦ **Bring stories to life.** Imagine and enact the voices of characters in a story you are reading together.

✦ **Move to the music.** Listen to various types of music and create movements that respond to each, or do some finger-painting with shaving cream to various "mood-music" recordings.

✦ **Draw it out.** Help your child draw or paint what he thinks happiness or sadness or a nightmare looks like.

✦ **Shake, rattle, and roll.** Use sticks, shakers, and kitchen utensils to create your own rhythm band.

✦ **Play the poetry game.** Take turns writing rhyming lines.

✦ **Groove to the music.** Turn on the tunes and have a dance fest!

ARTISTIC APPRECIATION

Some third-graders may not be active artists themselves, but they will watch other people create and appreciate others' creative products and processes. Third-graders are able to understand that the colors, lines, shapes, sounds, movements, and facial expressions that artists make are ways of speaking or expressing ideas. They can think and talk about what the creator or performer was trying to communicate.

FROM SCHOOL TO HOME

At school your child can watch a classmate paint or sculpt and give compliments or make comments: "It looks like you are trying to make this a happy picture." He can also enjoy the artwork of fellow students displayed in the school's entryway. He'll attentively listen and watch musical or dramatic performances. He can understand, for example, that the clown or the magician who performed at school is an artist communicating in his or her own special way. His appreciation of literature will be expressed as he writes a review of a book and includes comments about the author's style of writing.

Your eight-year-old has likely developed a preference for a particular kind of music. He probably notices the ways dancers are able to twist and turn their bodies. He'll express his artistic tastes by making comments about the artwork he sees in a book or in a store or museum. He may compliment a sibling or friend on her artwork. Don't be surprised if he comments about the statue on the town green or in a photograph and talks about the difficulty and skill needed to create such a piece.

"Because I usually find it difficult to discuss music or art, I especially like the suggestions of questions I can ask my child: For example, 'What do you think the artist was trying to communicate?'"

It's Your Turn

To help him develop artistic insight:

+ **Follow the art.** Take your child to view artworks at local art shows, flea markets, craft fairs, and antique shops.

+ **Discuss what you see.** Talk with your child about the things a work of art makes you think of; wonder if the artist had a thought he was trying to communicate.

+ **See a live show.** Attend a concert or play with your child, and comment on the skills displayed by the performers.

+ **See a film.** Go to a movie with your child and discuss: what you and he liked most about the movie; what motivated the main character; what the message of the film was, if there was one.

+ **Interpret tones.** Listen to a variety of music with your child and discuss: what the music makes you both think of; how it makes you feel; if there was a mood or feeling you thought the composer was trying to communicate.

+ **Hear instrumental "voices."** Talk with your child about the instruments used in an instrumental tape or CD or in a marching band.

+ **Discuss the orchestra.** Talk about the various groups of instruments (wind, string, percussion, and so on).

+ **Discuss the players.** Talk about the ways different instruments, from a harmonica to a grand piano, are played and the special skills of the musicians who play them.

+ **Cruise crafts.** Go to an arts-and-crafts fair with your child and spend time watching the different types of artists at work, such as potters, weavers, painters, and wood carvers.

+ **Read up on art.** Check out from the library some children's books about famous artists, musicians, or dancers.

+ **Notice book art.** When you read with your child, comment on the art style of the illustrator and begin to compare one style of illustration with another.

+ **Watch for fine design.** Notice and comment on striking creativity in dress designs, home landscaping, the colors in a bed spread, the design of next year's car; build an appreciation for the artistry in so many things people buy and use.

CHAPTER 22

Physical Development and Health

✦

In third grade physical development is enhanced by children's ability to move with greater speed, accuracy, and agility. By this time children are able to integrate their physical skills into sports, gymnastics, and dance. Their fine motor skills have also developed so that it is easier for them to write as well as to create work that shows more attention to detail and control.

Eight-year-olds can also be more responsible about taking care of their bodies and learning about nutrition, the importance of adequate rest, the effects of smoking, and the use of alcohol or drugs. Personal hygiene is also becoming more meaningful for them. Third-graders' physical development and personal health and safety can be seen in three areas:

Large-muscle development

Small-muscle development

Personal health and safety

LARGE-MUSCLE DEVELOPMENT

Third-graders are strong, energetic, and continually on the move. It's wonderful to see them flash through a room or across a playground, avoiding obstacles and quickly changing directions without slowing down. Also impressive is their ability to coordinate more than one movement at a time.

FROM SCHOOL TO HOME

School provides children with plenty of space and occasions for movement. Your eight-year-old moves or dances to songs that she sings. She performs basic tumbling maneuvers, such as cartwheels and flips. At recess she plays active physical games, such as kickball, softball, or soccer. She also does jump-rope tricks with friends.

At home your child easily carries many things at once without dropping or spilling. She can now move large boxes or pieces of furniture. She'll run and play active games or sports for long periods of time, as well as try daring physical challenges, such as jumping from heights, walking narrow surfaces, and performing bicycle tricks. You may see her become quite skilled at a particular sport, such as swimming, track, or bowling.

It's Your Turn

To motivate your child to move, move, move:

+ **Get physical with her.** Make sure active play is part of your everyday schedule.

+ **Stay fit together.** Exercise with your child by going jogging or walking.

+ **Catch it.** Try playing catch with a ball or throwing a Frisbee with your child.

+ **Overcome obstacles.** Set up a challenging obstacle course in your house or yard for your child to maneuver through. Create a variety of new challenges together.

+ **Turn on the tape.** Try exercising to a videotape with her.

+ **Encourage extracurricular action.** Help your child get involved in organized sports or recreation activities.

+ **Join her in meditative moves.** Establish a relaxation-exercise routine together; consider yoga or Tai Chi.

+ **Get to work!** Do outside chores with your child: raking leaves, shoveling snow, clearing brush, stacking wood, gardening, building—and have fun doing it together.

+ **Work on your technique.** Try some special skill-building activities with your child, such as playing baseball, bowling, jumping rope, or even line dancing.

+ **Stretch it out.** Do a few minutes of morning stretching exercises together; get into modern-dance or ballet stretches for a bit of artistic structure in your moves.

SMALL-MUSCLE DEVELOPMENT

By the time children are in the third grade, the small muscles in their fingers, hands, and wrists are well-developed. They have good control of their movements, even when working with very small objects. They can coordinate their eyes and hands, which allows them to carry out precise activities like threading a needle, using a hand drill or hammer, or writing clearly and neatly.

FROM SCHOOL TO HOME

Your third-grader's hands are kept very busy in school. He may make special signs, posters, or title pages by writing fancy letters. He's beginning to use cursive writing. Your child can thread a needle to make a string of tiny beads in an intricate pattern. He may use tweezers to remove a scale from a fish and place the scale on a microscope slide to study. He also may use the computer keyboard when finishing a report that is to be "published."

He uses his home computer with speed and accuracy. And he writes notes in smaller, more neatly formed letters than just a year ago. He's able to build intricate models of airplanes, vehicles, or buildings, and he may play the piano or other musical instrument. Your child may ask you for help, for instance, to sew pieces into a quilt for his pet's bed.

"This book has given me so many ways to help my children learn to persevere, even when they make mistakes."

It's Your Turn

To keep his fingers nimble:

+ **Have him tell a visual story.** Suggest that your child draw pictures about family events and then caption them with a short story that describes the work.

+ **Teach him to sew for himself.** Start simple sewing projects with your child, such as making cross-stitching around his pillow case or embroidering his initials on a T-shirt.

+ **Do paper work.** Help your child create folded paper objects, such as hats, boats, or paper boxes.

+ **Build model airplanes or cars together.**

+ **Be carpenters.** Do some woodworking with your child, such as building a simple bookcase for his room.

+ **Tie it up in knots.** Try knot-tying with your child; find a library book that shows many different kinds of knots that are used for specific purposes.

+ **Have him do "handy" work.** Encourage your child to develop finger dexterity by peeling vegetables, pouring milk and juice for himself and others, tying his little sister's shoes, or folding the laundry.

+ **Play with your fingers.** Play games with him that require dexterity, such as "Pick-Up-Sticks," cards, jacks, checkers, marbles, or "Tiddly Winks."

+ **Applaud his skill.** Praise your child's efforts to do detailed work even when it isn't perfect.

+ **Get him to slow down.** Encourage your child to work more slowly when doing detailed work—third-graders have a tendency to rush.

PERSONAL HEALTH AND SAFETY

Third-graders understand they can't take health and safety for granted. They know the difference between nutritious food and "junk" food (although they don't always make healthy choices!). They know when they are tired and when their bodies need rest. They know that cleanliness helps them stay healthy.

FROM SCHOOL TO HOME

Your child learns about personal health from a variety of school activities. She studies the human body and specific organs—lungs, heart, kidneys. She understands the food pyramid and is able to identify foods that fall into the protein, carbohydrate, and fat categories. She and her classmates identify and discuss unsafe and unhealthy activities, such as smoking, drinking too much alcohol, and abusing drugs. She also learns basic first-aid skills and how to act during fire drills.

You have encouraged your child to follow good hygiene rules. That means she washes her hands after using the toilet, before meals, and when helping with the cooking or setting the table. In addition, she is in the habit of brushing her teeth after meals and at bedtime. Your eight-year-old knows to treat a wound or bruise with ice, first-aid cream, and a bandage. She wears a bicycle helmet and a car seat belt without being reminded, and she knows how to cross the street safely.

"This book provides wonderful ideas to help children learn good health and safety practices."

It's Your Turn

To help your child take care of herself:

+ **Stay healthy and safe yourself.** Model good habits and practices as an example for your child.

+ **Eat smart.** Make healthy, nutritious foods available, and discuss the food groups when planning or cooking family meals.

+ **Raise a smart chef.** Let your child help plan and prepare healthy meals.

+ **Mind the meds.** Teach your child respect for and safe, appropriate use of medicines, vitamins, and over-the-counter drugs.

+ **Have family fire drills.**

+ **Let her monitor the detector.** Give your child the job of changing the batteries in the smoke detector; remind her to replace batteries twice a year (the days you change the clocks in spring and fall are good times for this).

+ **Drill bike-helmet safety.** Make sure your child wears a helmet each time she rides her bike. Let her know that most serious bike injuries occur when kids don't wear helmets.

+ **Buckle up.** Make sure you and all passengers have your seat belts buckled before you start the car. When you make it a habit, your child will, too.

+ **Do some pre–driver's ed.** Talk with your child about safe, defensive driving when she is riding with you in the car.

+ **Raise a substance-free kid.** Discuss health hazards, such as smoking, alcohol, and drugs. Encourage her to act on what she knows is safe and healthy instead of what she may see other kids doing. Reassure her that she can always talk to you about anything that she finds frightening or uncomfortable.

Looking Ahead

◆

As this book ends, your child is looking forward eagerly to fourth grade—to new subjects to learn, new discoveries to make, and new friends to meet. Because of your involvement, your child knows that learning does not stop at the classroom door. His family creates a learning environment at home where he, and everyone in the family, continues to learn every day.

Parents are a child's first teacher. We hope that this book has helped you turn everyday activities into enjoyable discoveries that add to your child's store of knowledge, challenge her imagination, and build her character. Learning for your child and you is what it should be—a rich and rewarding part of daily life.

Along the way, we hope that you have discovered a great deal about your child's unique gifts, interests, and talents, and that you have found countless ways to nurture them. We have tried to help you come up with inventive ways to build interest and skills that will give your child an extra boost.

We encourage you to continue this approach so that the bridge between home and school remains strong. Many of the activities you share with your child in the years and months ahead may not be new. They may just be variations of what you are currently doing. But, today's favorites can spark new ideas. Be open to them and enjoy learning and discovering with your child.

Over time, your child will also be able to participate increasingly in some of your own hobbies and favorite pastimes. These make for great learning opportunities. They also help you build shared interests and close bonds with your child.

Children's pride and joy in themselves knows no bounds when they make a new discovery or master a new skill. By continuing to use the activities and approach of this book, you are helping to create countless numbers of such "winning" situations. These experiences are invaluable for your child, and they are rewarding and fun for you and everyone else involved.

Keep on with the good practices you have set in place and the relationship you are continuing to strengthen. You are building a strong foundation for your child's life and learning, And you are creating priceless memories for the years to come.

Our best wishes to you and your family.

Sam Meisels, Charlotte Stetson, and Dot Marsden

About the Authors

$\blacklozenge$

Samuel J. Meisels, Ed.D. is a professor of education and a research scientist at the University of Michigan. He is widely regarded as the nation's leading authority on the assessment of young children. He has pioneered the development of alternative assessment strategies, including the *Work Sampling System*® on which *Winning Ways to Learn* is based. These strategies have been used successfully by tens of thousands of teachers nationwide for over a decade to keep track of how children learn and develop. Because of their effectiveness in assisting teachers  and in measuring achievement, these strategies are now mandated for young children in a number of states throughout the country.

Major areas of Dr. Meisels's professional commitment include: *developing alternative assessment strategies; the impact of standardized tests on young children; early identification of disability and risk conditions in early childhood; and developmental consequences of high-risk birth.*

Dr. Meisels has published more than 100 articles, books, and monographs in the fields of early childhood development and education, assessment, and special education. He serves as a consultant to numerous state departments of education, government agencies, private research institutes, and foundations. He is the president-elect of the Board of Zero to Three: The National Center for Infants, Toddlers and Families and has held senior advisory positions with many organizations including the National Academy of Sciences and Head Start.

Charlotte Stetson, M.Ed., is a leading developer of educational programs for young children, and has worked extensively with teachers on developmentally-appropriate curriculum, instruction, and assessment. A former first and second grade teacher, she is a contributing author to the teaching materials for the *Work Sampling System*®. She has co-authored books for teachers about curriculum development and is an author of a book for parents designed to help their children learn math skills, entitled *You Can Count on Mother Goose.*

Dorothea B. Marsden, M.Ed., is a nationally-known early childhood educator, trainer, and developer of assessments for preschoolers and school-age children. She has helped design and direct numerous innovative, high quality early childhood programs in Massachusetts and Vermont. She is a consultant to the national Early Head Start program and was one of the primary authors and professional developers for the *Work Sampling System*®. She is the co-author of the *Early Screening Inventory·Revised*® and additional assessment materials.

About the
Work Sampling System ®

The *Work Sampling System*® is an authentic performance assessment that provides an alternative to group-administered, norm-referenced achievement tests in preschool through fifth grade. Its purpose is to document and assess children's skills, knowledge, behavior, and accomplishments across a wide variety of curriculum areas on multiple occasions.

The *Work Sampling System* consists of three complementary elements:

1) Development Guidelines and Checklists

2) Portfolios of children's work

3) Summary Reports

Assessments based on the *Work Sampling* approach take place three times a year. They are designed to reflect classroom goals and objectives and to help teachers keep track of children's continuous progress by placing their work within a broad, developmental perspective. Through its focus on documenting individual performance of classroom-based tasks, *Work Sampling* enhances student motivation, assists teachers in instructional decision-making, and serves as an effective means for reporting children's progress to families, professional educators, and the community.

For more information, please call (800) 435-3085
or access www.rebusinc.com.